THE CLEAN POWER PLAN'S ECONOMIC IMPACT

STATE BY STATE

By Wayne Winegarden, Ph.D
and Alexander Specht

THE CLEAN POWER PLAN'S ECONOMIC IMPACT
STATE BY STATE

By Wayne Winegarden, Ph.D and Alexander Specht

ISBN: 978-1-934276-29-7

Pacific Research Institute
101 Montgomery Street, Suite 1300
San Francisco, CA 94104

Tel: 415-989-0833
Fax: 415-989-2411
www.pacificresearch.org

Download copies of this study at www.pacificresearch.org.

Contents

Introduction 7

Alabama...............................9

Arizona................................11

Arkansas..............................13

California 15

Colorado 17

Connecticut...........................19

Delaware 21

Florida................................23

Georgia 25

Idaho..................................27

Illinois 29

Indiana................................31

Iowa 33

Kansas 35

Kentucky..............................37

Louisiana 39

Maine.................................41

Maryland..............................43

Massachusetts 45

Michigan...............................47

Minnesota.............................49

Mississippi............................51

Missouri...............................53

Montana...............................55

Nebraska 57

Nevada................................59

New Hampshire 61

New Jersey............................63

New Mexico 65

New York..............................67

North Carolina........................69

North Dakota..........................71

Ohio 73

Oklahoma 75

Oregon 77

Pennsylvania..........................79

Rhode Island 81

South Carolina 83

South Dakota 85

Tennessee............................87

Texas.................................89

Utah 91

Vermont 93

Virginia................................95

Washington...........................97

West Virginia..........................99

Wisconsin 101

Wyoming..............................103

About the Authors...............106

About PRI............................107

Introduction

This addendum to The Clean Power Plan's Economic Impact shows detailed results for the 48 contiguous states.

For each state, the findings present four different expenditure burdens:

1. The current average annual electricity costs relative to 2014 median household income (cost burden) by neighborhood (formally U.S. Census Tracts);

2. The impact on the electricity cost burden by neighborhood if the Clean Power Plan (CPP) is implemented, and consumers do not change their behavior;

3. The impact on the electricity cost burden by neighborhood if the CPP is implemented and consumers economize on their consumption based on the estimated short-term behavioral responses; and

4. The impact on the electricity burden by neighborhood if the CPP is implemented and consumers economize on their consumption based on the estimated long-term behavioral responses.

Detailed state maps are provided for each of the four expenditure burdens.

County-level information by state can be accessed via an interactive map online at pacificresearch.org

Alabama

As of 2014, the average annual expenditures on electricity in Alabama were $1,745, or 4.13 percent of the 2014 median household income of $42,278. The cost burden ranges from a low of 1.43 percent in parts of Jefferson County (median household income of $135,417), to a high of 13.73 percent in parts of Mobile County (median household income of $8,579)

2014 EXPENDITURES AS
A PERCENTAGE OF
MEDIAN HOUSEHOLD INCOME

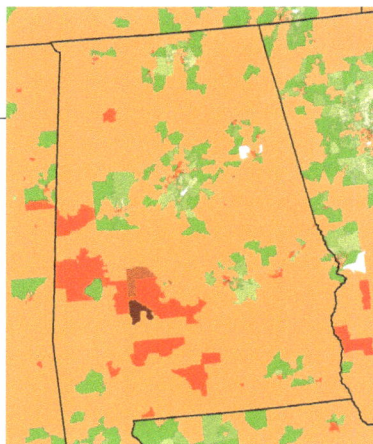

If the CPP is implemented, and consumers do not change their behavior, the cost burden will increase significantly to an average of $2,159 or 5.11 percent of 2014 median household income. In the high-income parts of Jefferson County, the burden increases to 1.77 percent, while in the low-income parts of Mobile County the burden increases to 16.99 percent.

EXPENDITURES AS A PERCENTAGE
OF MEDIAN HOUSEHOLD INCOME:
STATIC ANALYSIS

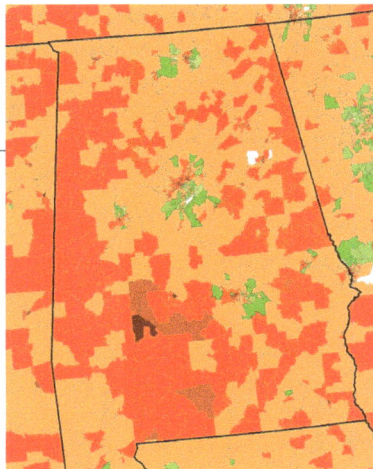

"Affordable energy, as we all know, is a vital necessity for every Alabama household and business alike; it is the cornerstone of a vibrant U.S. economy."

—Testimony of Blaine Galliher Alabama Gov. Robert Bentley's Administration in opposition to CPP

FACT

Under the Obama Clean Power Plan, average electricity expenditures would equal 16.99 percent of the income of the poorest families in Mobile County.

LEGEND

- 0.9% and below
- 0.9% to 1.4%
- 1.4% to 1.8%
- 1.8% to 2.2%
- 2.2% to 2.6%
- 2.6% to 3.0%
- 3.0% to 5.0%
- 5.0% to 7.5%
- 7.5% to 10%
- 10% and above
- Other

If consumers economize on their electricity consumption following the implementation of the CPP, then the cost burden will increase but by less than under the static scenario. Based on the historical response in the short-term, average expenditures will increase to $2,049 or 4.85 percent of 2014 median household income − 1.68 percent in parts of Jefferson County and 16.12 percent in parts of Mobile County.

EXPENDITURES AS A
PERCENTAGE OF MEDIAN
HOUSEHOLD INCOME:
SHORT-TERM

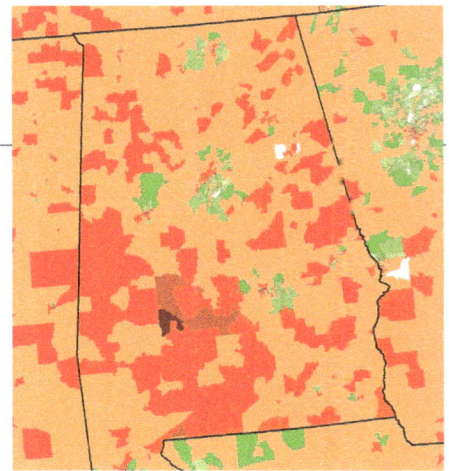

Based on the historical response in the long-term, average expenditures will increase to $1,903 or 4.50 percent of 2014 median household income − 1.56 percent in parts of Jefferson County and 14.98 percent in parts of Mobile County

EXPENDITURES AS A
PERCENTAGE OF MEDIAN
HOUSEHOLD INCOME:
LONG-TERM

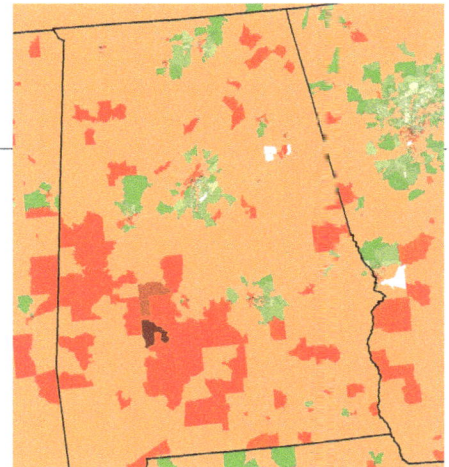

LEGEND

- 0.9% and below
- 0.9% to 1.4%
- 1.4% to 1.8%
- 1.8% to 2.2%
- 2.2% to 2.6%
- 2.6% to 3.0%
- 3.0% to 5.0%
- 5.0% to 7.5%
- 7.5% to 10%
- 10% and above
- Other

Arizona

As of 2014, the average annual expenditures on electricity in Arizona were $1,428, or 2.90 percent of the 2014 median household income of $49,254. The cost burden ranges from a low of 0.89 percent in parts of Maricopa County (median household income of $177,778), to a high of 10.15 percent in other parts of Maricopa County (median household income of $9,500).

2014 EXPENDITURES AS A
PERCENTAGE OF MEDIAN
HOUSEHOLD INCOME

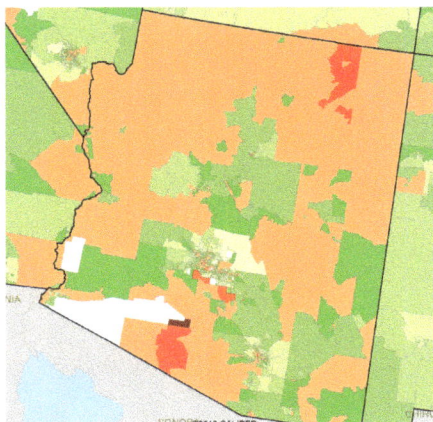

If the CPP is implemented, and consumers do not change their behavior, the cost burden will increase significantly to an average of $1,592 or 3.23 percent of 2014 median household income. In the high-income parts of Maricopa County, the burden increases to 0.99 percent, while in the low-income parts of Maricopa County the burden increases to 11.32 percent.

EXPENDITURES AS A
PERCENTAGE OF MEDIAN
HOUSEHOLD INCOME: STATIC
ANALYSIS

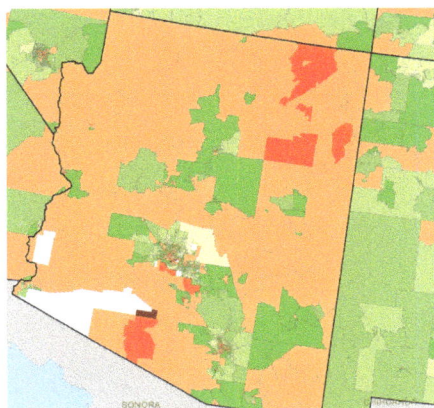

FACT

Low-income residents in the Phoenix area could spend nearly $1,600 a year for electricity under the Obama climate change agenda.

LEGEND

- 0.9% and below
- 0.9% to 1.4%
- 1.4% to 1.8%
- 1.8% to 2.2%
- 2.2% to 2.6%
- 2.6% to 3.0%
- 3.0% to 5.0%
- 5.0% to 7.5%
- 7.5% to 10%
- 10% and above
- Other

If consumers economize on their electricity consumption following the implementation of the CPP, the cost burden will increase but by less than under the static scenario. Based on the historical response in the short-term, average expenditures will increase to $1,558 or 3.16 percent of 2014 median household income – 0.97 percent in parts of Maricopa County and 11.07 percent in parts of Maricopa County.

EXPENDITURES AS A
PERCENTAGE OF MEDIAN
HOUSEHOLD INCOME:
SHORT-TERM

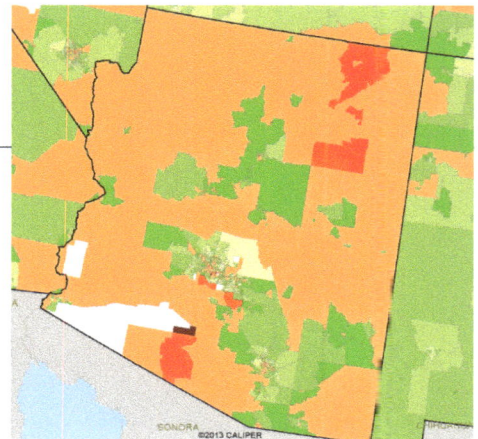

Based on the historical response in the long-term, average expenditures will increase to $1,549 or 3.14 percent of 2014 median household income – 0.96 percent in the upper-income parts of Maricopa County and 11.01 percent in the lower-income parts of Maricopa County.

LEGEND

	0.9% and below
	0.9% to 1.4%
	1.4% to 1.8%
	1.8% to 2.2%
	2.2% to 2.6%
	2.6% to 3.0%
	3.0% to 5.0%
	5.0% to 7.5%
	7.5% to 10%
	10% and above
	Other

EXPENDITURES AS A
PERCENTAGE OF MEDIAN
HOUSEHOLD INCOME:
LONG-TERM

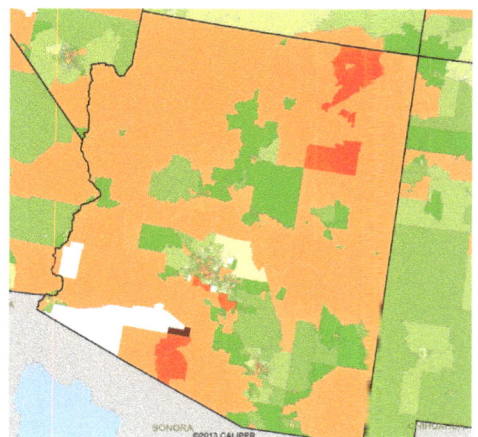

Arkansas

As of 2014, the average annual expenditures on electricity in Arkansas were $1,302, or 2.90 percent of the 2014 median household income of $44,922. The cost burden ranges from a low of 0.92 percent in parts of Pulaski County (median household income of $156,680), to a high of 6.32 percent in parts of Miller County (median household income of $13,899).

2014 EXPENDITURES AS A PERCENTAGE OF MEDIAN HOUSEHOLD INCOME

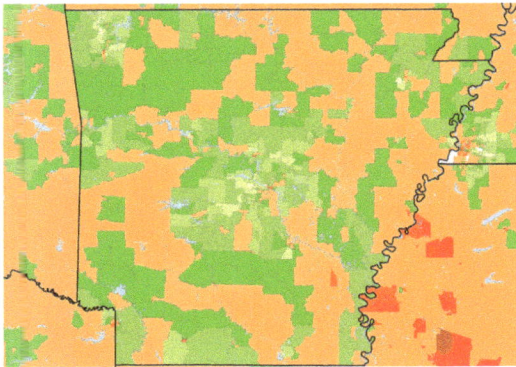

If the CPP is implemented, and consumers do not change their behavior, the cost burden will increase significantly to an average of $1,601 or 3.56 percent of 2014 median household income. In the high-income parts of Pulaski County, the burden increases to 1.13 percent, while in the low-income parts of Miller County the burden increases to 7.78 percent.

EXPENDITURES AS A PERCENTAGE OF MEDIAN HOUSEHOLD INCOME: STATIC ANALYSIS

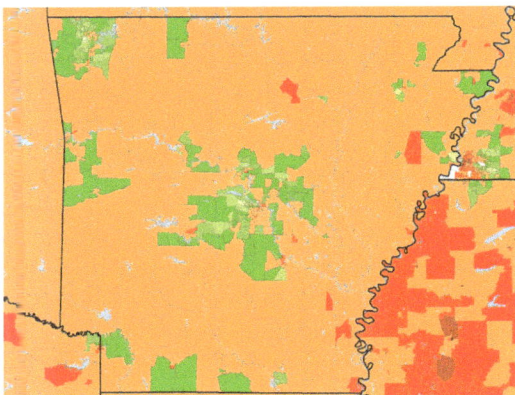

"It is clear that the Obama administration's Clean Power Plan could still result in significant electric rate increases for middle-class ratepayers while having a minimal impact on global temperatures."

—Gov. Asa Hutchinson

FACT

Average electricity expenditures under the Obama climate agenda could soon equal nearly 8 percent of the income of Arkansas' poorest families in Miller County.

LEGEND

- 0.9% and below
- 0.9% to 1.4%
- 1.4% to 1.8%
- 1.8% to 2.2%
- 2.2% to 2.6%
- 2.6% to 3.0%
- 3.0% to 5.0%
- 5.0% to 7.5%
- 7.5% to 10%
- 10% and above
- Other

If consumers economize on their electricity consumption following the implementation of the CPP, the cost burden will increase but by less than under the static scenario. Based on the historical response in the short-term, average expenditures will increase to $1,563 or 3.48 percent of 2014 median household income – 1.11 percent in parts of Pulaski County and 7.59 percent in parts of Miller County.

EXPENDITURES AS A PERCENTAGE OF MEDIAN HOUSEHOLD INCOME: SHORT-TERM

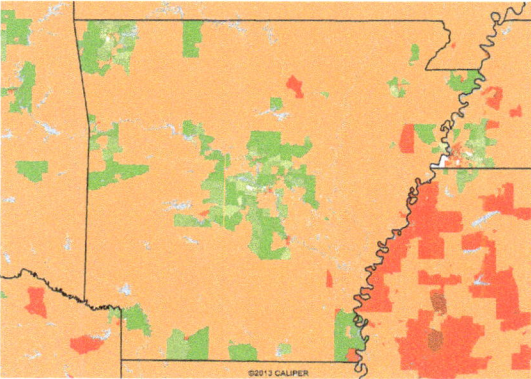

Based on the historical response in the long-term, average expenditures will increase to $1,549 or 3.45 percent of 2014 median household income – 1.10 percent in the upper-income parts of Pulaski County and 7.53 percent in the lower-income parts of Miller County.

EXPENDITURES AS A PERCENTAGE OF MEDIAN HOUSEHOLD INCOME: LONG-TERM

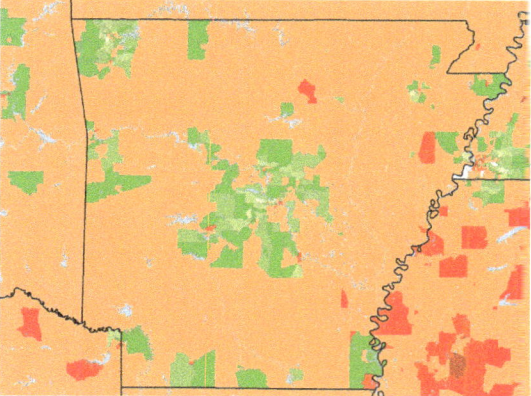

LEGEND

- 0.9% and below
- 0.9% to 1.4%
- 1.4% to 1.8%
- 1.8% to 2.2%
- 2.2% to 2.6%
- 2.6% to 3.0%
- 3.0% to 5.0%
- 5.0% to 7.5%
- 7.5% to 10%
- 10% and above
- Other

California

As of 2014, the average annual expenditures on electricity in California were $1,083, or 1.79 percent of the 2014 median household income of $60,487. The cost burden ranges from a low of 0.59 percent in parts of San Mateo County (median household income of at least $250,000), to a high of 15.87 percent in parts of San Luis Obispo County (median household income of at least $4,607).

2014 EXPENDITURES AS A
PERCENTAGE OF MEDIAN
HOUSEHOLD INCOME

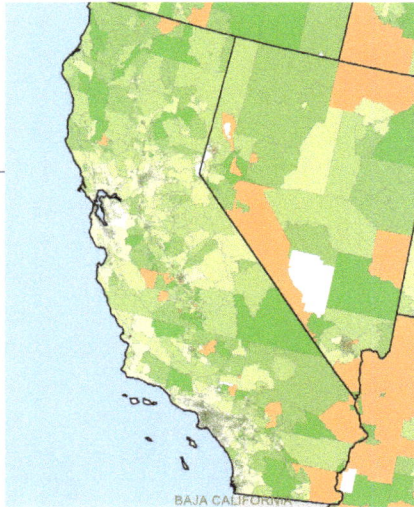

If the CFP is implemented, and consumers do not change their behavior, the cost burden will increase significantly to an average of $1,185 or 1.96 percent of 2014 median household income. In the high-income parts of San Mateo County, the burden increases to 0.64 percent, while in the low-income parts of San Luis Obispo County the burden increases to 17.36 percent.

EXPENDITURES AS A
PERCENTAGE OF MEDIAN
HOUSEHOLD INCOME:
STATIC ANALYSIS

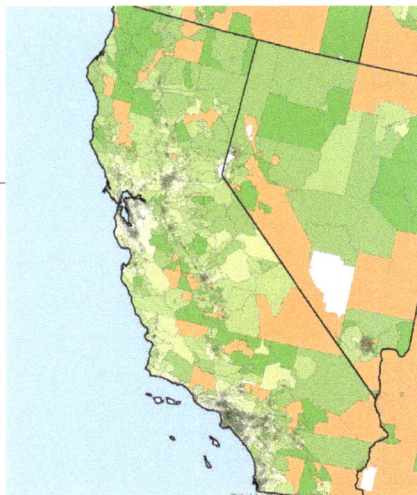

"there is a regressive nature to some of these things,'... 'We have to be sensitive to issues relating to energy costs.'"

—Gavin Newsom
California Lt. Governor

FACTS

- For poor residents of San Luis Obispo County, average electricity expenditures could soon equal 17.36 percent of their income if the Clean Power Plan takes effect.

- On average, Californians could pay nearly $1,200 a year for electricity under the Clean Power Plan.

- Riverside County residents could see their annual electricity bills rise by 9.0 percent under the Clean Power Plan. Kern County residents could see their costs rise by 8.9 percent.

LEGEND

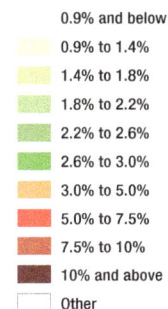

0.9% and below
0.9% to 1.4%
1.4% to 1.8%
1.8% to 2.2%
2.2% to 2.6%
2.6% to 3.0%
3.0% to 5.0%
5.0% to 7.5%
7.5% to 10%
10% and above
Other

If consumers economize on their electricity consumption following the implementation of the CPP, the cost burden will increase but by less than under the static scenario. Based on the historical response in the short-term, average expenditures will increase to $1,165 or 1.93 percent of 2014 median household income – 0.63 percent in parts of San Mateo County and 17.08 percent in parts of San Luis Obispo County.

EXPENDITURES AS A PERCENTAGE OF MEDIAN HOUSEHOLD INCOME: SHORT-TERM

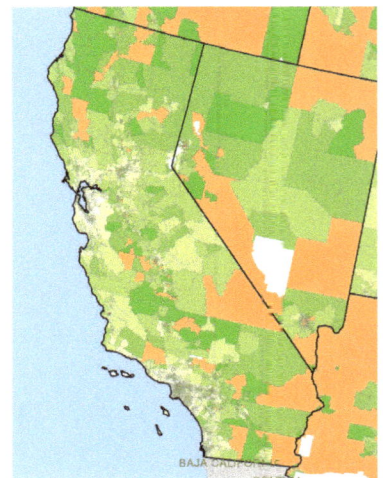

Based on the historical response in the long-term, average expenditures will increase to $1,159 or 1.92 percent of 2014 median household income – 0.63 percent in the upper-income parts of San Mateo County and 16.98 percent in the lower-income parts of San Luis Obispo County.

EXPENDITURES AS A PERCENTAGE OF MEDIAN HOUSEHOLD INCOME: LONG-TERM

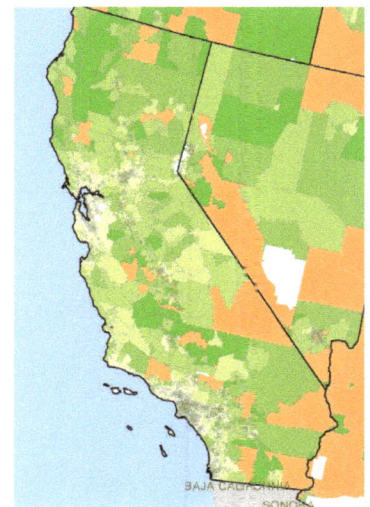

LEGEND

- 0.9% and below
- 0.9% to 1.4%
- 1.4% to 1.8%
- 1.8% to 2.2%
- 2.2% to 2.6%
- 2.6% to 3.0%
- 3.0% to 5.0%
- 5.0% to 7.5%
- 7.5% to 10%
- 10% and above
- Other

Colorado

As of 2014, the average annual expenditures on electricity in Colorado were $998, or 1.64 percent of the 2014 median household income of $60,940. The cost burden ranges from a low of 0.54 percent in parts of Arapahoe County (median household income of at least $250,000), to a high of 7.19 percent in parts of Denver County (median household income of $9,363).

2014 EXPENDITURES AS A PERCENTAGE OF MEDIAN HOUSEHOLD INCOME

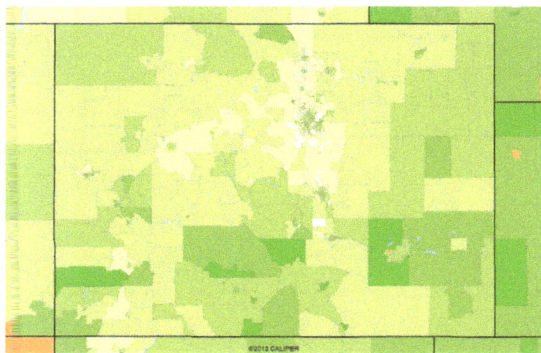

If the CPP is implemented, and consumers do not change their behavior, the cost burden will increase significantly to an average of $1,190 or 1.95 percent of 2014 median household income. In the high-income parts of Arapahoe County, the burden increases to 0.65 percent, while in the low-income parts of Denver County the burden increases to 8.58 percent.

EXPENDITURES AS A PERCENTAGE OF MEDIAN HOUSEHOLD INCOME: STATIC ANALYSIS

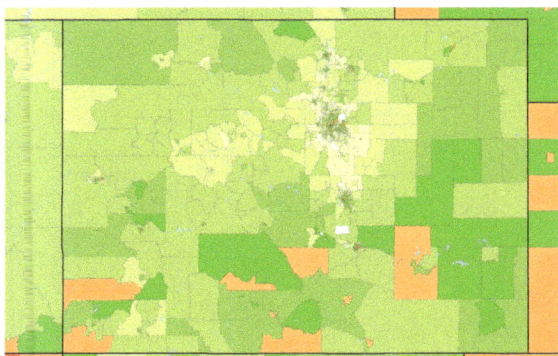

FACTS

- Poor families in Denver County could see average electricity expenditures equal 8.58 percent of their household income under the Clean Power Plan.

- Colorado residents could soon be paying $1,190 a year on average for electricity if the new clean power regulations from Washington take effect.

- Dolores County residents could see their electricity costs rise by 16.6 percent.

LEGEND

- 0.9% and below
- 0.9% to 1.4%
- 1.4% to 1.8%
- 1.8% to 2.2%
- 2.2% to 2.6%
- 2.6% to 3.0%
- 3.0% to 5.0%
- 5.0% to 7.5%
- 7.5% to 10%
- 10% and above
- Other

If consumers economize on their electricity consumption following the implementation of the CPP, the cost burden will increase but by less than under the static scenario. Based on the historical response in the short-term, average expenditures will increase to $1,149 or 1.89 percent of 2014 median household income − 0.62 percent in parts of Arapahoe County and 8.29 percent in parts of Denver County.

EXPENDITURES AS A PERCENTAGE OF MEDIAN HOUSEHOLD INCOME: SHORT-TERM

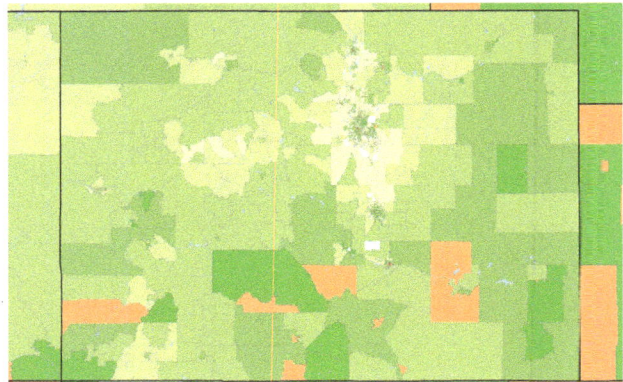

Based on the historical response in the long-term, average expenditures will increase to $1,139 or 1.87 percent of 2014 median household income − 0.62 percent in the upper-income parts of Arapahoe County and 8.21 percent in the lower-income parts of Denver County.

EXPENDITURES AS A PERCENTAGE OF MEDIAN HOUSEHOLD INCOME: LONG-TERM

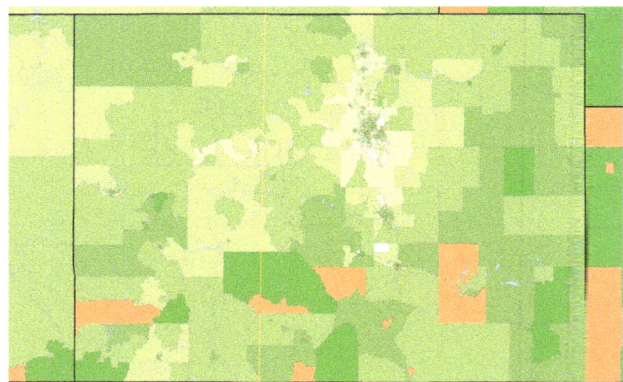

LEGEND

	0.9% and below
	0.9% to 1.4%
	1.4% to 1.8%
	1.8% to 2.2%
	2.2% to 2.6%
	2.6% to 3.0%
	3.0% to 5.0%
	5.0% to 7.5%
	7.5% to 10%
	10% and above
	Other

Connecticut

As of 2014, the average annual expenditures on electricity in Connecticut were $1,571, or 2.24 percent of the 2014 median household income of $70,161. The cost burden ranges from a low of 0.85 percent in parts of Fairfield County (median household income of at least $250,000), to a high of 9.43 percent in parts of New Haven County (median household income of $11,254).

2014 EXPENDITURES AS A PERCENTAGE OF MEDIAN HOUSEHOLD INCOME

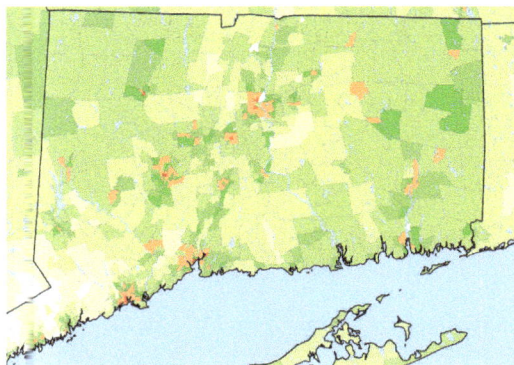

If the CPP is implemented, and consumers do not change their behavior, the cost burden will increase significantly to an average of $1,824 or 2.60 percent of 2014 median household income. In the high-income parts of Fairfield County, the burden increases to 0.99 percent, while in the low-income parts of New Haven County the burden increases to 10.94 percent.

EXPENDITURES AS A PERCENTAGE OF MEDIAN HOUSEHOLD INCOME: STATIC ANALYSIS

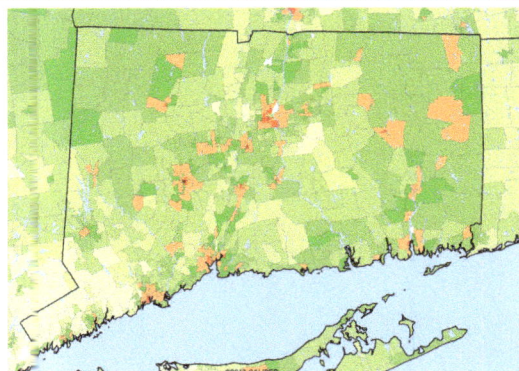

LEGEND

- 0.9% and below
- 0.9% to 1.4%
- 1.4% to 1.8%
- 1.8% to 2.2%
- 2.2% to 2.6%
- 2.6% to 3.0%
- 3.0% to 5.0%
- 5.0% to 7.5%
- 7.5% to 10%
- 10% and above
- Other

If consumers economize on their electricity consumption following the implementation of the CPP, the cost burden will increase but by less than under the static scenario. Based on the historical response in the short-term, average expenditures will increase to $1,776 or 2.53 percent of 2014 median household income − 0.96 percent in parts of Fairfield County and 10.65 percent in parts of New Haven County.

EXPENDITURES AS A PERCENTAGE OF MEDIAN HOUSEHOLD INCOME: SHORT-TERM

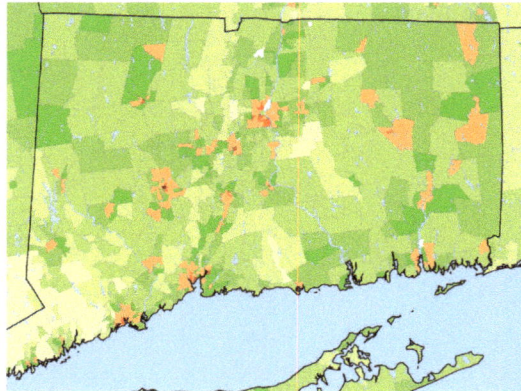

Based on the historical response in the long-term, average expenditures will increase to $1,742 or 2.48 percent of 2014 median household income − 0.95 percent in the upper-income parts of Fairfield County and 10.45 percent in the lower-income parts of New Haven County.

EXPENDITURES AS A PERCENTAGE OF MEDIAN HOUSEHOLD INCOME: LONG-TERM

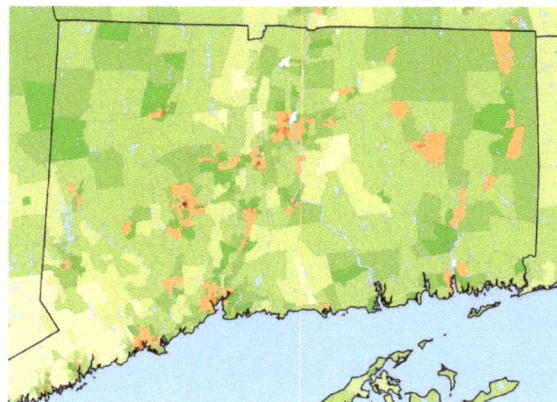

LEGEND

	0.9% and below
	0.9% to 1.4%
	1.4% to 1.8%
	1.8% to 2.2%
	2.2% to 2.6%
	2.6% to 3.0%
	3.0% to 5.0%
	5.0% to 7.5%
	7.5% to 10%
	10% and above
	Other

Delaware

As of 2014, the average annual expenditures on electricity in Delaware were $1,494, or 2.60 percent of the 2014 median household income of $57,522. The cost burden ranges from a low of 1.06 percent in parts of New Castle County (median household income of $156,050), to a high of 8.47 percent in other parts of New Castle County (median household income of $11,910).

2014 EXPENDITURES AS A PERCENTAGE OF MEDIAN HOUSEHOLD INCOME

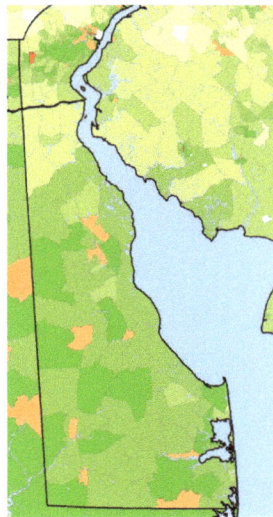

If the CPP is implemented, and consumers do not change their behavior, the cost burden will increase significantly to an average of $1,830 or 3.18 percent of 2014 median household income. In the high-income parts of New Castle County, the burden increases to 1.30 percent, while in the low-income parts of New Castle County the burden increases to 10.37 percent.

EXPENDITURES AS A PERCENTAGE OF MEDIAN HOUSEHOLD INCOME: STATIC ANALYSIS

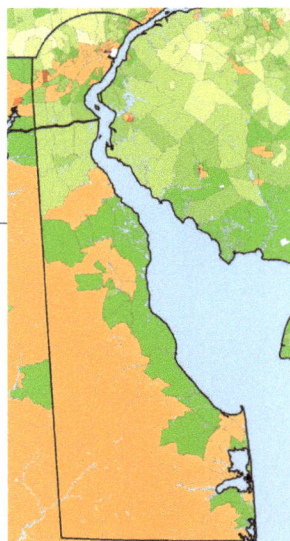

FACTS

- Low-income residents in New Castle County could soon see their average electricity expenditures increase to 10.37 percent of their income under the Clean Power Plan.

- On average, Delaware families could be spending $1,830 annually for electricity if the new Washington regulations take effect.

- New Castle County residents could see their electricity costs rise by 18.3 percent under the Plan.

LEGEND

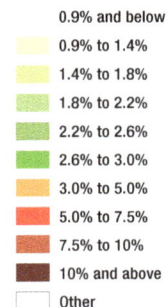

0.9% and below
0.9% to 1.4%
1.4% to 1.8%
1.8% to 2.2%
2.2% to 2.6%
2.6% to 3.0%
3.0% to 5.0%
5.0% to 7.5%
7.5% to 10%
10% and above
Other

If consumers economize on their electricity consumption following the implementation of the CPP, the cost burden will increase but by less than under the static scenario. Based on the historical response in the short-term, average expenditures will increase to $1,723 or 2.99 percent of 2014 median household income – 1.22 percent in parts of New Castle County and 9.77 percent in other parts of New Castle County.

EXPENDITURES AS A PERCENTAGE OF MEDIAN HOUSEHOLD INCOME: SHORT-TERM

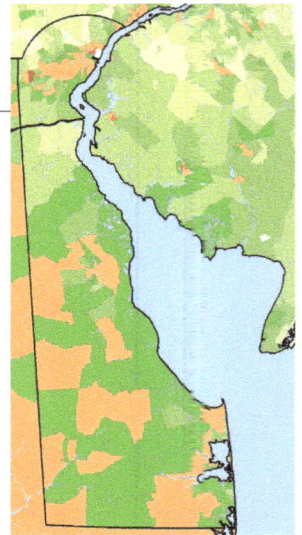

Based on the historical response in the long-term, average expenditures will increase to $1,711 or 2.97 percent of 2014 median household income – 1.21 percent in the upper-income parts of New Castle County and 9.70 percent in the lower-income parts of New Castle County.

EXPENDITURES AS A PERCENTAGE OF MEDIAN HOUSEHOLD INCOME: LONG-TERM

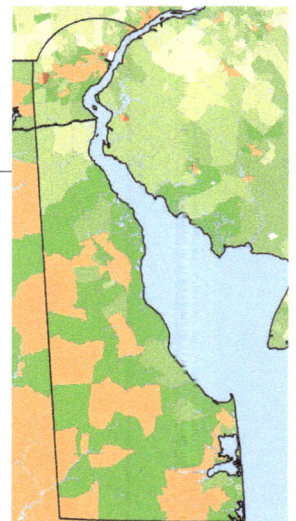

LEGEND

- 0.9% and below
- 0.9% to 1.4%
- 1.4% to 1.8%
- 1.8% to 2.2%
- 2.2% to 2.6%
- 2.6% to 3.0%
- 3.0% to 5.0%
- 5.0% to 7.5%
- 7.5% to 10%
- 10% and above
- Other

Florida

As of 2014, the average annual expenditures on electricity in Florida were $1,559, or 3.38 percent of the 2014 median household income of $46,140. The cost burden ranges from a low of 0.85 percent in parts of Miami-Dade County (median household income of at least $250,000), to a high of 28.31 percent in Hillsborough County (median household income of $3,717).

2014 EXPENDITURES AS A PERCENTAGE OF MEDIAN HOUSEHOLD INCOME

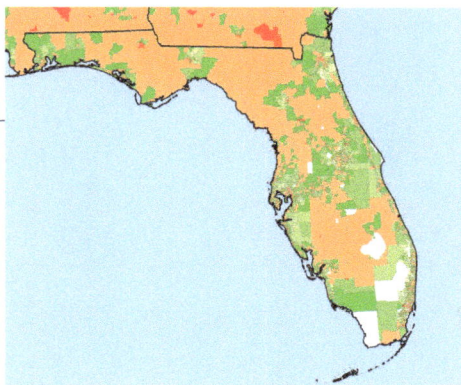

If the CPP is implemented, and consumers do not change their behavior, the cost burden will increase significantly to an average of $1,870 or 4.05 percent of 2014 median household income. In the high-income parts of Miami-Dade County, the burden increases to 1.02 percent, while in the low-income parts of Hillsborough County the burden increases to 33.97 percent.

EXPENDITURES AS A PERCENTAGE OF MEDIAN HOUSEHOLD INCOME: STATIC ANALYSIS

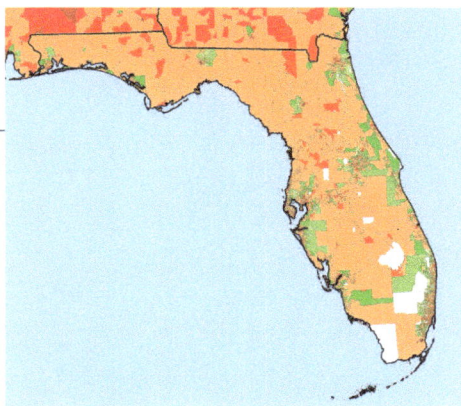

"We need policies that are good for our natural environment, but also good for our economy. The Obama Administration's Clean Power Plan would devastate our economy and increase the cost of living for millions of American families already struggling with high bills and expenses. In Florida alone, these irresponsible regulations could raise individual electric bills significantly."

—Senator Marco Rubio

FACT

Florida's poorest families in Hillsborough County could soon see average electricity expenditures rise to 34 percent of their income under the Obama climate agenda.

LEGEND

- 0.9% and below
- 0.9% to 1.4%
- 1.4% to 1.8%
- 1.8% to 2.2%
- 2.2% to 2.6%
- 2.6% to 3.0%
- 3.0% to 5.0%
- 5.0% to 7.5%
- 7.5% to 10%
- 10% and above
- Other

If consumers economize on their electricity consumption following the implementation of the CPP, the cost burden will increase but by less than under the static scenario. Based on the historical response in the short-term, average expenditures will increase to $1,771 or 3.84 percent of 2014 median household income – 0.96 percent in parts of Miami-Dade and 32.17 percent in parts of Hillsborough County.

EXPENDITURES AS A
PERCENTAGE OF MEDIAN
HOUSEHOLD INCOME:
SHORT-TERM

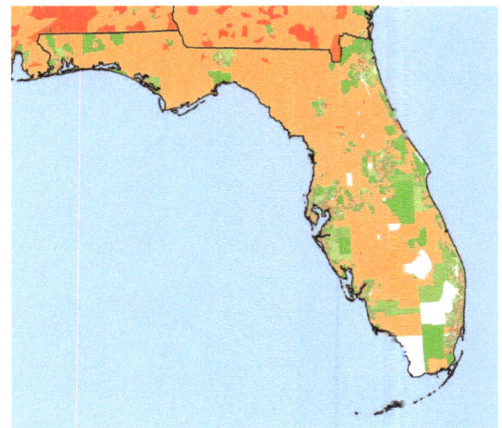

Based on the historical response in the long-term, average expenditures will increase to $1,761 or 3.82 percent of 2014 median household income – 0.96 percent in the upper-income parts of Miami-Dade and 31.98 percent in the lower-income parts of Hillsborough County.

EXPENDITURES AS A
PERCENTAGE OF MEDIAN
HOUSEHOLD INCOME:
LONG-TERM

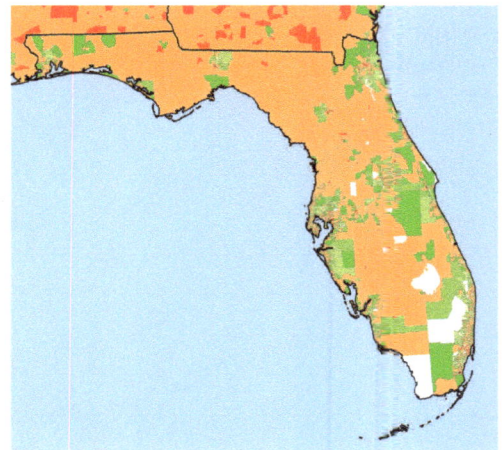

LEGEND

- 0.9% and below
- 0.9% to 1.4%
- 1.4% to 1.8%
- 1.8% to 2.2%
- 2.2% to 2.6%
- 2.6% to 3.0%
- 3.0% to 5.0%
- 5.0% to 7.5%
- 7.5% to 10%
- 10% and above
- Other

Georgia

As of 2014, the average annual expenditures on electricity in Georgia were $1,610, or 3.25 percent of the 2014 median household income of $49,555. The cost burden ranges from a low of 1.01 percent in parts of Fulton County (median household income of $176,615), to a high of 43.49 percent in other parts of Fulton County (median household income of at least $2,500).

2014 EXPENDITURES AS A
PERCENTAGE OF MEDIAN
HOUSEHOLD INCOME

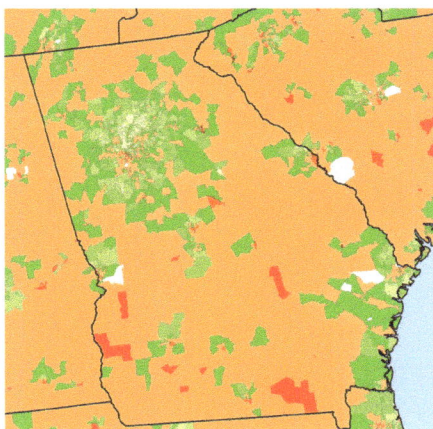

If the CPP is implemented, and consumers do not change their behavior, the cost burden will increase significantly to an average of $1,973 or 3.98 percent of 2014 median household income. In the high-income parts of Fulton County, the burden increases to 1.24 percent, while in the low-income parts of Fulton County the burden increases to 53.28 percent.

EXPENDITURES AS A
PERCENTAGE OF MEDIAN
HOUSEHOLD INCOME:
STATIC ANALYSIS

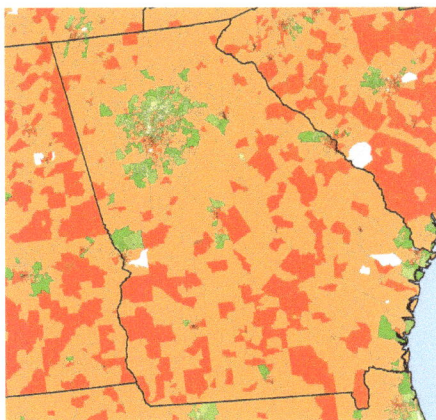

"The damaging effects . . . will drive up energy prices for Georgia families and businesses, while the ripple effect throughout our economy will increase costs of basic necessities for those already struggling to make ends meet."

—Senator David Perdue

FACT

Georgia's poorest residents in the Atlanta area could soon see average electricity expenditures rise to 53 percent of their income under the Obama Clean Power plan.

LEGEND

- 0.9% and below
- 0.9% to 1.4%
- 1.4% to 1.8%
- 1.8% to 2.2%
- 2.2% to 2.6%
- 2.6% to 3.0%
- 3.0% to 5.0%
- 5.0% to 7.5%
- 7.5% to 10%
- 10% and above
- Other

If consumers economize on their electricity consumption following the implementation of the CPP, the cost burden will increase but by less than under the static scenario. Based on the historical response in the short-term, average expenditures will increase to $1,858 or 3.75 percent of 2014 median household income – 1.17 percent in parts of Fulton County and 50.16 percent in other parts of Fulton County.

EXPENDITURES AS A PERCENTAGE OF MEDIAN HOUSEHOLD INCOME: SHORT-TERM

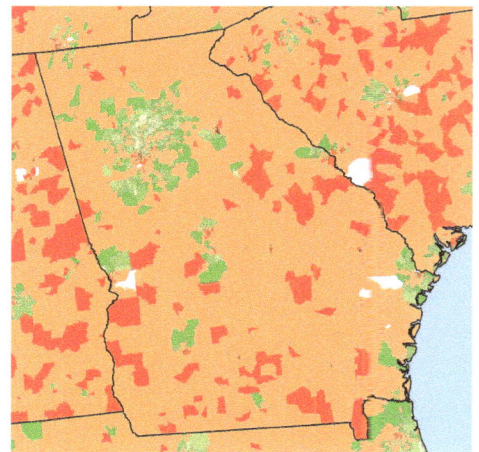

Based on the historical response in the long-term, average expenditures will increase to $1,845 or 3.72 percent of 2014 median household income – 1.16 percent in the upper-income parts of Fulton County and 49.83 percent in the lower-income parts of Fulton County.

EXPENDITURES AS A PERCENTAGE OF MEDIAN HOUSEHOLD INCOME: LONG-TERM

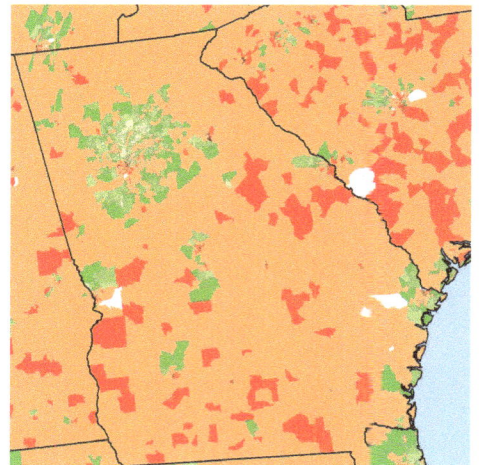

LEGEND

	0.9% and below
	0.9% to 1.4%
	1.4% to 1.8%
	1.8% to 2.2%
	2.2% to 2.6%
	2.6% to 3.0%
	3.0% to 5.0%
	5.0% to 7.5%
	7.5% to 10%
	10% and above
	Other

Idaho

As of 2014, the average annual expenditures on electricity in Idaho were $1,146, or 2.15 percent of the 2014 median household income of $53,438. The cost burden ranges from a low of 1.04 percent in parts of Ada County (median household income of $122,500), to a high of 5.20 percent in parts of Canyon County (median household income of at least $14,889).

2014 EXPENDITURES AS A
PERCENTAGE OF MEDIAN HOUSEHOLD
INCOME

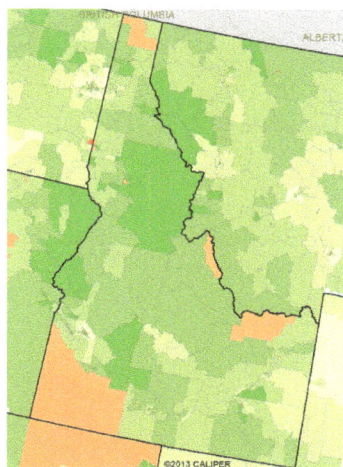

If the CPP is implemented, and consumers do not change their behavior, the cost burden will increase significantly to an average of $1,338 or 2.50 percent of 2014 median household income. In the high-income parts of Ada County, the burden increases to 1.21 percent, while in the low-income parts of Canyon County the burden increases to 6.07 percent.

EXPENDITURES AS A PERCENTAGE OF
MEDIAN HOUSEHOLD INCOME:
STATIC ANALYSIS

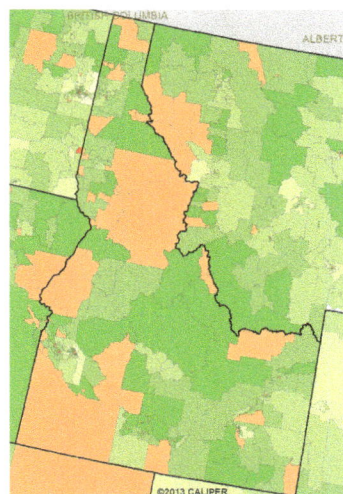

LEGEND

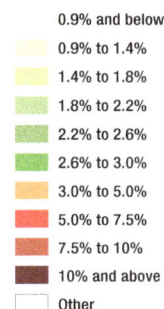

0.9% and below
0.9% to 1.4%
1.4% to 1.8%
1.8% to 2.2%
2.2% to 2.6%
2.6% to 3.0%
3.0% to 5.0%
5.0% to 7.5%
7.5% to 10%
10% and above
Other

If consumers economize on their electricity consumption following the implementation of the CPP, the cost burden will increase but by less than under the static scenario. Based on the historical response in the short-term, average expenditures will increase to $1,297 or 2.43 percent of 2014 median household income – 1.17 percent in parts of Ada County and 5.88 percent in parts of Canyon County.

EXPENDITURES AS A PERCENTAGE OF
MEDIAN HOUSEHOLD INCOME:
SHORT-TERM

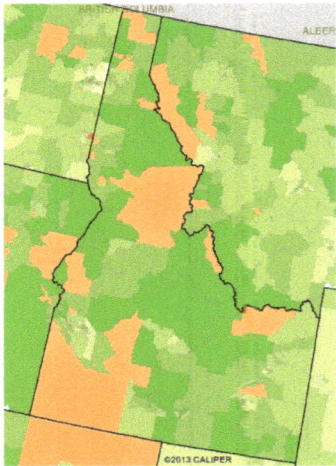

Based on the historical response in the long-term, average expenditures will increase to $1,287 or 2.41 percent of 2014 median household income – 1.16 percent in the upper-income parts of Ada County and 5.83 percent in the lower-income parts of Canyon County.

EXPENDITURES AS A PERCENTAGE OF
MEDIAN HOUSEHOLD INCOME:
LONG-TERM

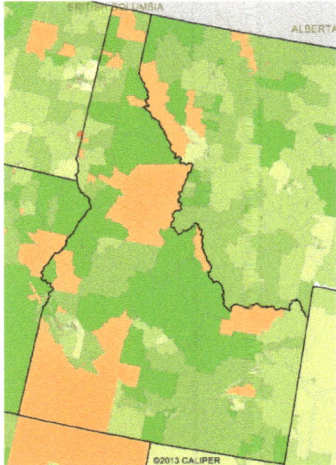

LEGEND

	0.9% and below
	0.9% to 1.4%
	1.4% to 1.8%
	1.8% to 2.2%
	2.2% to 2.6%
	2.6% to 3.0%
	3.0% to 5.0%
	5.0% to 7.5%
	7.5% to 10%
	10% and above
	Other

Illinois

As of 2014, the average annual expenditures on electricity in Illinois were $1,107, or 2.02 percent of the 2014 median household income of $54,916. The cost burden ranges from a low of 0.60 percent in parts of Cook County (median household income of at least $250,000), to a high of 18.03 percent in low-income parts of Cook County (median household income of $4,145).

2014 EXPENDITURES AS A PERCENTAGE OF MEDIAN HOUSEHOLD INCOME

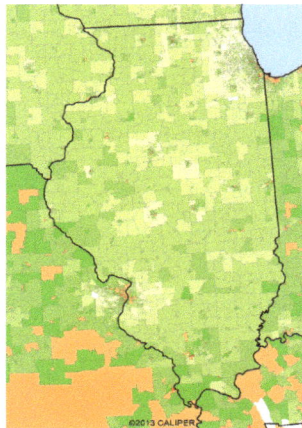

If the CPP is implemented, and consumers do not change their behavior, the cost burden will increase significantly to an average of $1,406 or 2.56 percent of 2014 median household income. In the high-income parts of Cook County, the burden increases to 0.76 percent, while in the low-income parts of Cook County the burden increases to 22.90 percent.

EXPENDITURES AS A PERCENTAGE OF MEDIAN HOUSEHOLD INCOME: STATIC ANALYSIS

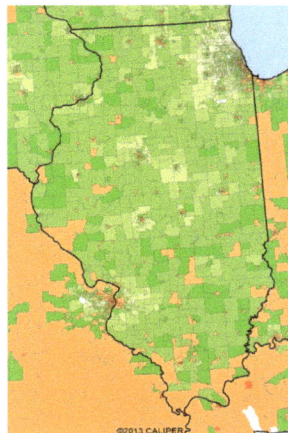

LEGEND

- 0.9% and below
- 0.9% to 1.4%
- 1.4% to 1.8%
- 1.8% to 2.2%
- 2.2% to 2.6%
- 2.6% to 3.0%
- 3.0% to 5.0%
- 5.0% to 7.5%
- 7.5% to 10%
- 10% and above
- Other

If consumers economize on their electricity consumption following the implementation of the CPP, the cost burden will increase but by less than under the static scenario. Based on the historical response in the short-term, average expenditures will increase to $1,357 or 2.47 percent of 2014 median household income – 0.74 percent in parts of Cook County and 22.11 percent in other parts of Cook County.

EXPENDITURES AS A PERCENTAGE OF
MEDIAN HOUSEHOLD INCOME:
SHORT-TERM

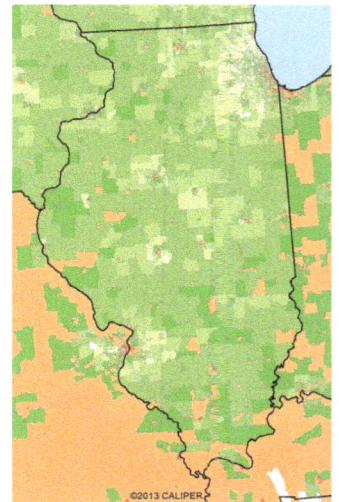

Based on the historical response in the long-term, average expenditures will increase to $1,333 or 2.43 percent of 2014 median household income – 0.72 percent in the upper-income parts of Cook County and 21.71 percent in the lower-income parts of Cook County.

EXPENDITURES AS A PERCENTAGE OF
MEDIAN HOUSEHOLD INCOME:
LONG-TERM

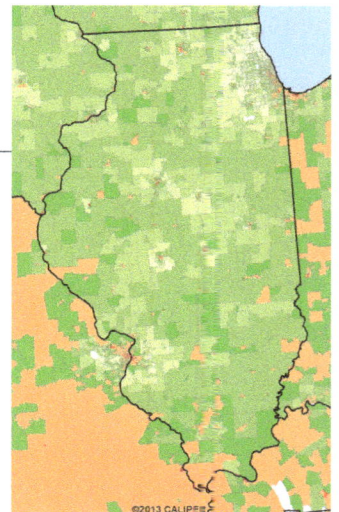

LEGEND

	0.9% and below
	0.9% to 1.4%
	1.4% to 1.8%
	1.8% to 2.2%
	2.2% to 2.6%
	2.6% to 3.0%
	3.0% to 5.0%
	5.0% to 7.5%
	7.5% to 10%
	10% and above
	Other

Indiana

As of 2014, the average annual expenditures on electricity in Indiana were $1,387, or 2.89 percent of the 2014 median household income of $48,060. The cost burden ranges from a low of 0.95 percent in parts of Hamilton County (median household income of $160,077), to a high of 29.08 percent in low-income parts of Tippecanoe County (median household income of $3,220).

2014 EXPENDITURES AS A PERCENTAGE OF MEDIAN HOUSEHOLD INCOME

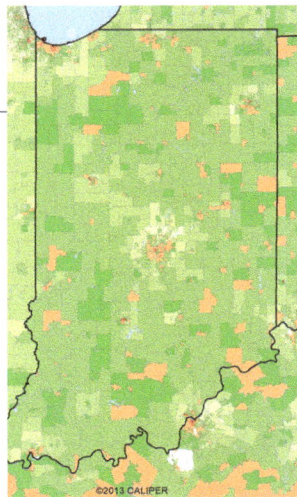

©2013 CALIPER

If the CPP is implemented, and consumers do not change their behavior, the cost burden will increase significantly to an average of $1,766 or 3.68 percent of 2014 median household income. In the high-income parts of Hamilton County, the burden increases to 1.21 percent, while in the low-income parts of Tippecanoe County the burden increases to 37.05 percent.

EXPENDITURES AS A PERCENTAGE OF MEDIAN HOUSEHOLD INCOME: STATIC ANALYSIS

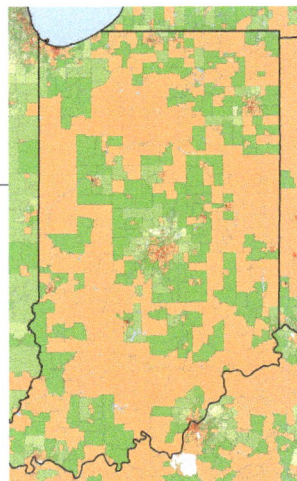

"The rule requires Hoosiers to carry one of the heaviest loads in reducing the country's carbon emissions, which will make energy more expensive for families and make it more difficult for Indiana businesses to compete."

—Senator
Joe Donnelly (D-IN)

FACT

Indiana's poorest families in Tippecanoe County could see average electricity expenditures rise to more than 37 percent of their income under the Obama Clean Power Plan.

LEGEND

	0.9% and below
	0.9% to 1.4%
	1.4% to 1.8%
	1.8% to 2.2%
	2.2% to 2.6%
	2.6% to 3.0%
	3.0% to 5.0%
	5.0% to 7.5%
	7.5% to 10%
	10% and above
	Other

If consumers economize on their electricity consumption following the implementation of the CPP, the cost burden will increase but by less than under the static scenario. Based on the historical response in the short-term, average expenditures will increase to $1,705 or 3.55 percent of 2014 median household income – 1.17 percent in parts of Hamilton County and 35.75 percent in parts of Tippecanoe County.

EXPENDITURES AS A PERCENTAGE OF
MEDIAN HOUSEHOLD INCOME:
SHORT-TERM

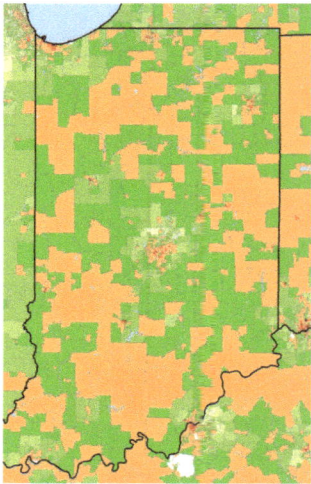

Based on the historical response in the long-term, average expenditures will increase to $1,674 or 3.48 percent of 2014 median household income – 1.15 percent in the upper-income parts of Hamilton County and 35.11 percent in the lower-income parts of Tippecanoe County.

EXPENDITURES AS A PERCENTAGE OF
MEDIAN HOUSEHOLD INCOME: LONG-TERM

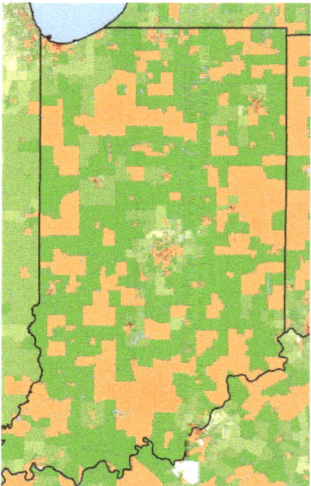

LEGEND

- 0.9% and below
- 0.9% to 1.4%
- 1.4% to 1.8%
- 1.8% to 2.2%
- 2.2% to 2.6%
- 2.6% to 3.0%
- 3.0% to 5.0%
- 5.0% to 7.5%
- 7.5% to 10%
- 10% and above
- Other

Iowa

As of 2014, the average annual expenditures on electricity in Iowa were $1,197, or 2.07 percent of the 2014 median household income of $57,810. The cost burden ranges from a low of 0.97 percent in parts of Dallas County (median household income of $137,188), to a high of 5.93 percent in low-income parts of Story County (median household income of $13,635).

2014 EXPENDITURES AS A PERCENTAGE OF MEDIAN HOUSEHOLD INCOME

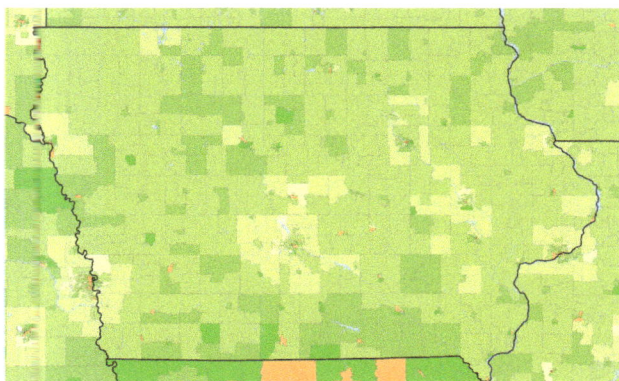

If the CPP is implemented, and consumers do not change their behavior, the cost burden will increase significantly to an average of $1,497 or 2.59 percent of 2014 median household income. In the high-income parts of Dallas County, the burden increases to 1.21 percent, while in the low-income parts of Story County the burden increases to 7.41 percent.

EXPENDITURES AS A PERCENTAGE OF MEDIAN HOUSEHOLD INCOME: STATIC ANALYSIS

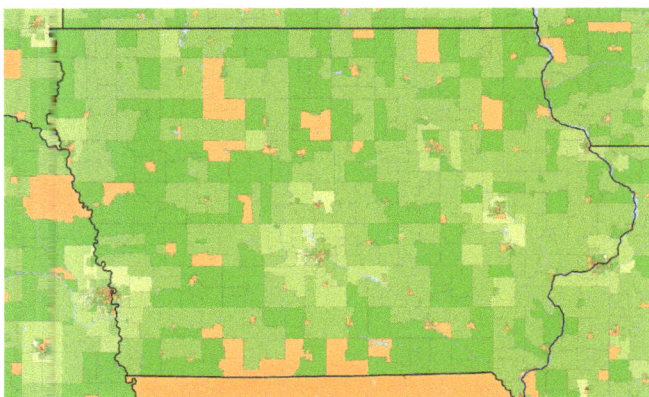

FACTS

- Iowa families could soon be paying nearly $1,500 on average for electricity under the Obama Administration's Clean Power Plan.

- Low-income families in Story County could face average electricity expenditures rising to 7.41 percent of their income if the new Washington regulations take effect.

- Appanoose County residents could see their annual power bills rise by 20.1 percent, while Buena Vista County residents could see theirs rise by 19.9 percent.

LEGEND

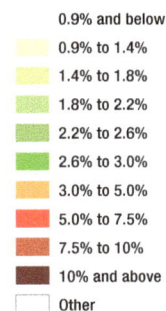

	0.9% and below
	0.9% to 1.4%
	1.4% to 1.8%
	1.8% to 2.2%
	2.2% to 2.6%
	2.6% to 3.0%
	3.0% to 5.0%
	5.0% to 7.5%
	7.5% to 10%
	10% and above
	Other

If consumers economize on their electricity consumption following the implementation of the CPP, the cost burden will increase but by less than under the static scenario. Based on the historical response in the short-term, average expenditures will increase to $1,448 or 2.50 percent of 2014 median household income – 1.17 percent in parts of Dallas County and 7.17 percent in parts of Story County.

EXPENDITURES AS A PERCENTAGE OF MEDIAN HOUSEHOLD INCOME: SHORT-TERM

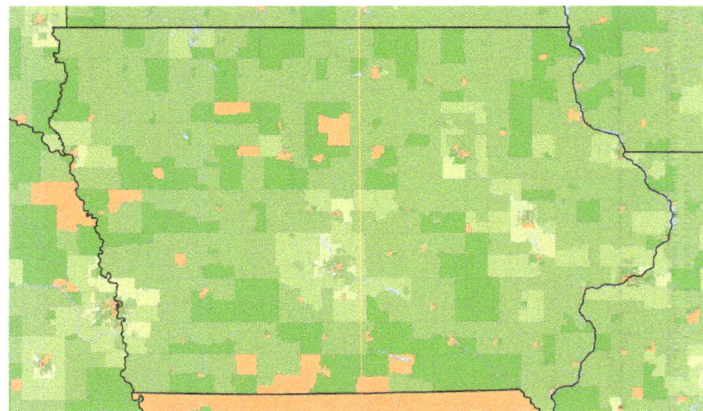

Based on the historical response in the long-term, average expenditures will increase to $1,424 or 2.46 percent of 2014 median household income – 1.15 percent in the upper-income parts of Dallas County and 7.05 percent in the lower-income parts of Story County.

LEGEND

	0.9% and below
	0.9% to 1.4%
	1.4% to 1.8%
	1.8% to 2.2%
	2.2% to 2.6%
	2.6% to 3.0%
	3.0% to 5.0%
	5.0% to 7.5%
	7.5% to 10%
	10% and above
	Other

EXPENDITURES AS A PERCENTAGE OF MEDIAN HOUSEHOLD INCOME: LONG-TERM

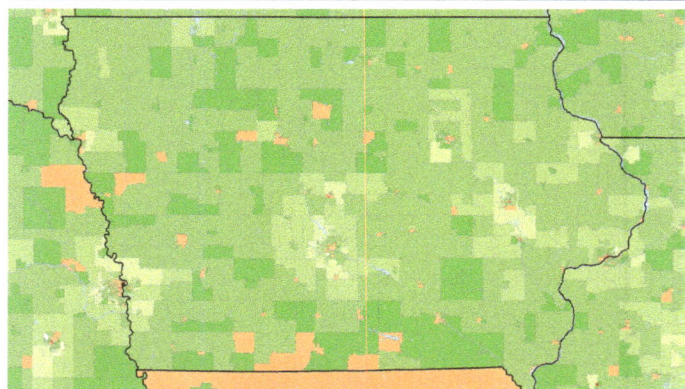

Kansas

As of 2014, the average annual expenditures on electricity in Kansas were $1,359, or 2.54 percent of the 2014 median household income of $53,444. The cost burden ranges from a low of 0.78 percent in parts of Johnson County (median household income of $192,292), to a high of 9.73 percent in low-income parts of Wyandotte County (median household income of $9,432).

2014 EXPENDITURES AS A PERCENTAGE OF MEDIAN HOUSEHOLD INCOME

If the CPP is implemented, and consumers do not change their behavior, the cost burden will increase significantly to an average of $1,704 or 3.19 percent of 2014 median household income. In the high-income parts of Johnson County, the burden increases to 0.98 percent, while in the low-income parts of Wyandotte County the burden increases to 12.20 percent.

EXPENDITURES AS A PERCENTAGE OF MEDIAN HOUSEHOLD INCOME: STATIC ANALYSIS

LEGEND

- 0.9% and below
- 0.9% to 1.4%
- 1.4% to 1.8%
- 1.8% to 2.2%
- 2.2% to 2.6%
- 2.6% to 3.0%
- 3.0% to 5.0%
- 5.0% to 7.5%
- 7.5% to 10%
- 10% and above
- Other

If consumers economize on their electricity consumption following the implementation of the CPP, the cost burden will increase but by less than under the static scenario. Based on the historical response in the short-term, average expenditures will increase to $1,648 or 3.08 percent of 2014 median household income – 0.95 percent in parts of Johnson County and 11.79 percent in parts of Wyandotte County.

EXPENDITURES AS A PERCENTAGE OF MEDIAN HOUSEHOLD INCOME: SHORT-TERM

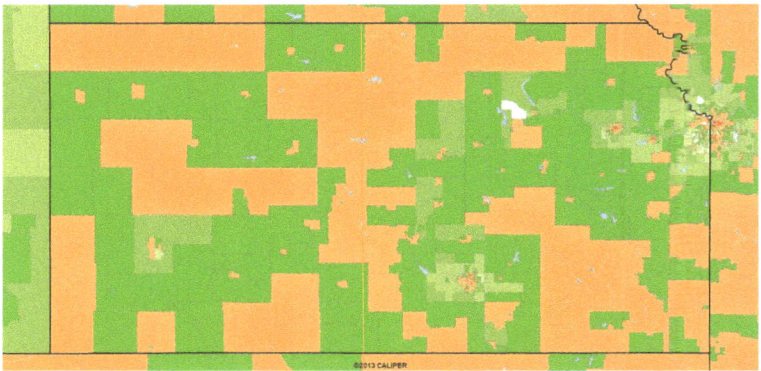

Based on the historical response in the long-term, average expenditures will increase to $1,620 or 3.03 percent of 2014 median household income – 0.93 percent in the upper-income parts of Johnson County and 11.59 percent in the lower-income parts of Wyandotte County.

EXPENDITURES AS A PERCENTAGE OF MEDIAN HOUSEHOLD INCOME LONG-TERM

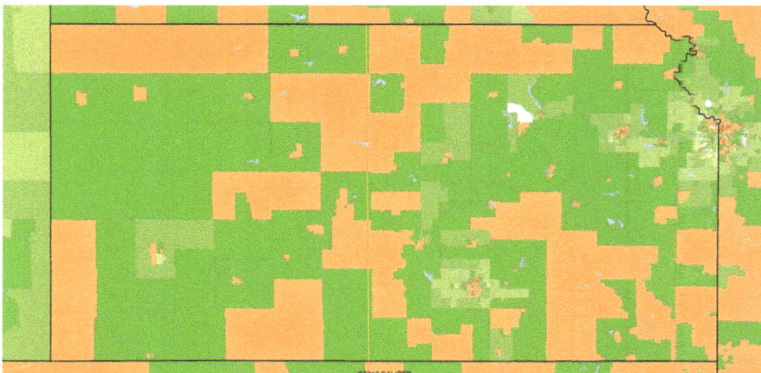

LEGEND

	0.9% and below
	0.9% to 1.4%
	1.4% to 1.8%
	1.8% to 2.2%
	2.2% to 2.6%
	2.6% to 3.0%
	3.0% to 5.0%
	5.0% to 7.5%
	7.5% to 10%
	10% and above
	Other

Kentucky

As of 2014, the average annual expenditures on electricity in Kentucky were $1,437, or 3.36 percent of the 2014 median household income of $42,786. The cost burden ranges from a low of 1.08 percent in parts of Oldham County (median household income of $147,250), to a high of 10.78 percent in low-income parts of Jefferson County (median household income of $9,003).

2014 EXPENDITURES AS A PERCENTAGE OF MEDIAN HOUSEHOLD INCOME

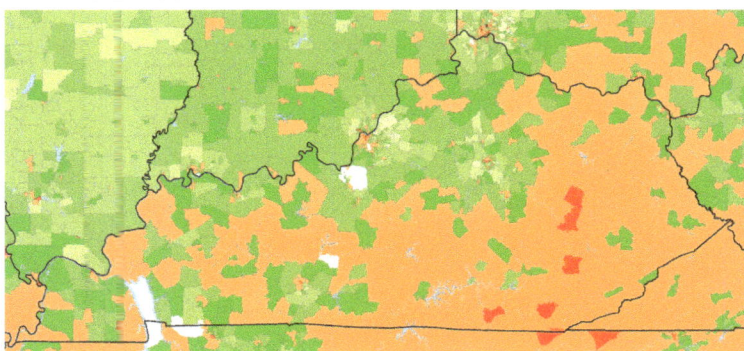

If the CPP is implemented, and consumers do not change their behavior, the cost burden will increase significantly to an average of $1,829 or 4.28 percent of 2014 median household income. In the high-income parts of Oldham County, the burden increases to 1.38 percent, while in the low-income parts of Jefferson County the burden increases to 13.72 percent.

EXPENDITURES AS A PERCENTAGE OF MEDIAN HOUSEHOLD INCOME: STATIC ANALYSIS

LEGEND

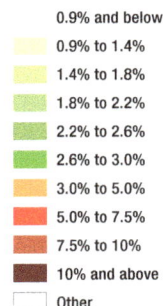

	0.9% and below
	0.9% to 1.4%
	1.4% to 1.8%
	1.8% to 2.2%
	2.2% to 2.6%
	2.6% to 3.0%
	3.0% to 5.0%
	5.0% to 7.5%
	7.5% to 10%
	10% and above
	Other

If consumers economize on their electricity consumption following the implementation of the CPP, the cost burden will increase but by less than under the static scenario. Based on the historical response in the short-term, average expenditures will increase to $1,725 or 4.03 percent of 2014 median household income − 1.30 percent in parts of Oldham County and 12.94 percent in parts of Jefferson County.

EXPENDITURES AS A PERCENTAGE OF MEDIAN HOUSEHOLD INCOME: SHORT-TERM

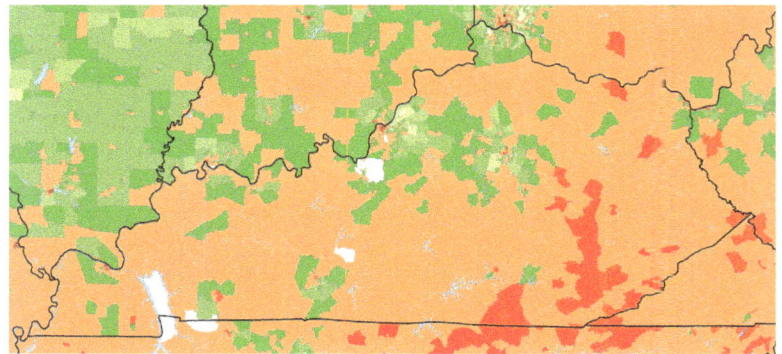

Based on the historical response in the long-term, average expenditures will increase to $1,587 or 3.71 percent of 2014 median household income − 1.19 percent in the upper-income parts of Oldham County and 11.90 percent in the lower-income parts of Jefferson County.

EXPENDITURES AS A PERCENTAGE OF MEDIAN HOUSEHOLD INCOME: LONG-TERM

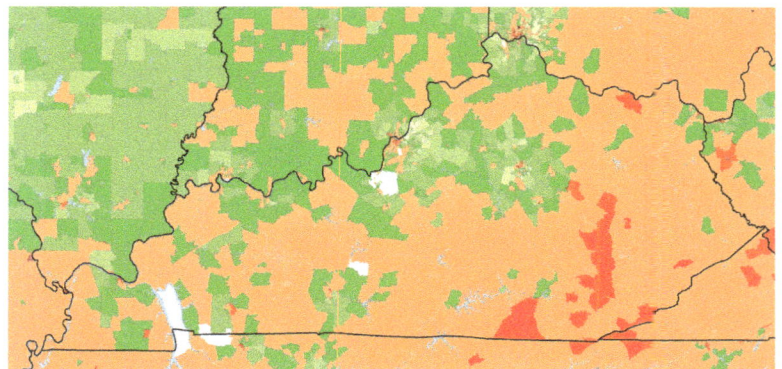

LEGEND

	0.9% and below
	0.9% to 1.4%
	1.4% to 1.8%
	1.8% to 2.2%
	2.2% to 2.6%
	2.6% to 3.0%
	3.0% to 5.0%
	5.0% to 7.5%
	7.5% to 10%
	10% and above
	Other

Louisiana

As of 2014, the average annual expenditures on electricity in Louisiana were $1,485, or 3.50 percent of the 2014 median household income of $42,406. The cost burden ranges from a low of 1.11 percent in parts of Orleans Parish (median household income of $148,281), to a high of 11.53 percent in low-income parts of Orleans Parish (median household income of $8,693).

2014 EXPENDITURES AS A PERCENTAGE OF MEDIAN HOUSEHOLD INCOME

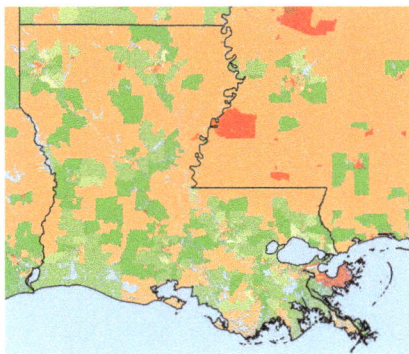

If the CPP is implemented, and consumers do not change their behavior, the cost burden will increase significantly to an average of $1,823 or 4.30 percent of 2014 median household income. In the high-income parts of Orleans Parish, the burden increases to 1.36 percent, while in the low-income parts of Orleans Parish the burden increases to 14.16 percent.

EXPENDITURES AS A PERCENTAGE OF MEDIAN HOUSEHOLD INCOME: STATIC ANALYSIS

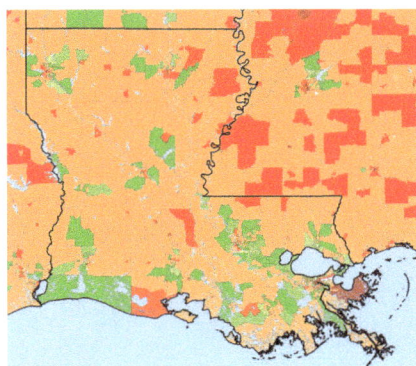

FACTS

- Louisiana residents could soon be paying $1,823 annual electricity bills on average if the Obama Clean Power Plan is implemented.

- Low-income families in Orleans Parish could soon face average electricity expenditures of 14.16 percent of their income under the new federal regulations.

- Residents in Allen and Catahoula Parishes could see their annual power bills rise by 18.7 percent.

LEGEND

0.9% and below
0.9% to 1.4%
1.4% to 1.8%
1.8% to 2.2%
2.2% to 2.6%
2.6% to 3.0%
3.0% to 5.0%
5.0% to 7.5%
7.5% to 10%
10% and above
Other

If consumers economize on their electricity consumption following the implementation of the CPP, the cost burden will increase but by less than under the static scenario. Based on the historical response in the short-term, average expenditures will increase to $1,780 or 4.20 percent of 2014 median household income – 1.33 percent in parts of Orleans Parish and 13.83 percent in parts of Orleans Parish.

EXPENDITURES AS A PERCENTAGE OF MEDIAN HOUSEHOLD INCOME SHORT-TERM

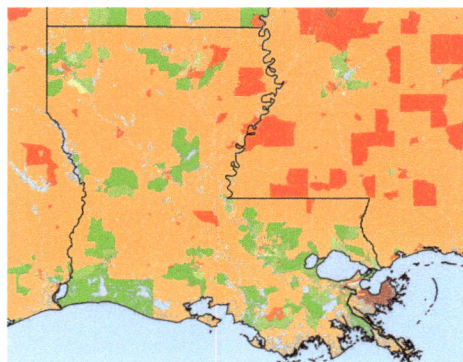

Based on the historical response in the long-term, average expenditures will increase to $1,765 or 4.16 percent of 2014 median household income – 1.32 percent in the upper-income parts of Orleans Parish and 13.70 percent in the lower-income parts of Orleans Parish.

EXPENDITURES AS A PERCENTAGE OF MEDIAN HOUSEHOLD INCOME: LONG-TERM

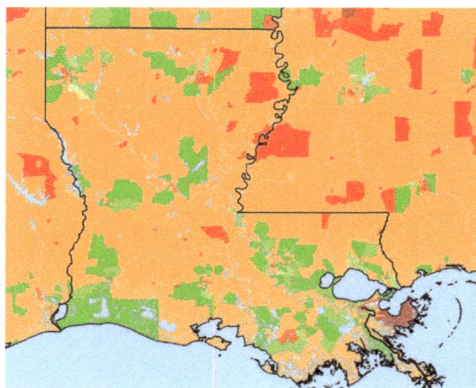

LEGEND

- 0.9% and below
- 0.9% to 1.4%
- 1.4% to 1.8%
- 1.8% to 2.2%
- 2.2% to 2.6%
- 2.6% to 3.0%
- 3.0% to 5.0%
- 5.0% to 7.5%
- 7.5% to 10%
- 10% and above
- Other

Maine

As of 2014, the average annual expenditures on electricity in Maine were $1,055, or 2.04 percent of the 2014 median household income of $51,710. The cost burden ranges from a low of 1.12 percent in parts of Cumberland County (median household income of $104,297), to a high of 5.45 percent in low-income parts of Androscoggin County (median household income of $13,074).

2014 EXPENDITURES AS A PERCENTAGE OF MEDIAN HOUSEHOLD INCOME

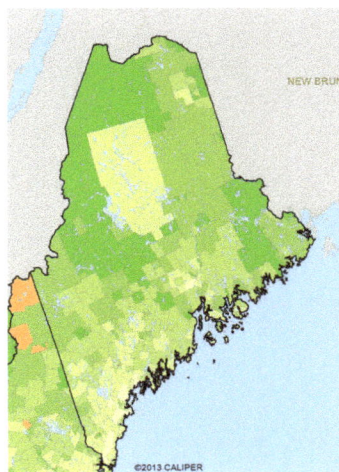

If the CPP is implemented, and consumers do not change their behavior, the cost burden will increase significantly to an average of $1,175 or 2.27 percent of 2014 median household income. In the high-income parts of Cumberland County, the burden increases to 1.25 percent, while in the low-income parts of Androscoggin County the burden increases to 6.07 percent.

EXPENDITURES AS A PERCENTAGE OF MEDIAN HOUSEHOLD INCOME: STATIC ANALYSIS

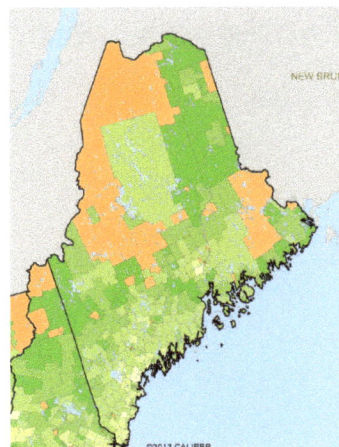

LEGEND

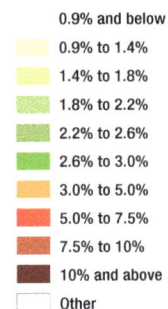

0.9% and below
0.9% to 1.4%
1.4% to 1.8%
1.8% to 2.2%
2.2% to 2.6%
2.6% to 3.0%
3.0% to 5.0%
5.0% to 7.5%
7.5% to 10%
10% and above
Other

If consumers economize on their electricity consumption following the implementation of the CPP, the cost burden will increase but by less than under the static scenario. Based on the historical response in the short-term, average expenditures will increase to $1,152 or 2.23 percent of 2014 median household income − 1.22 percent in parts of Cumberland County and 5.95 percent in parts of Androscoggin County.

EXPENDITURES AS A PERCENTAGE OF MEDIAN HOUSEHOLD INCOME: SHORT-TERM

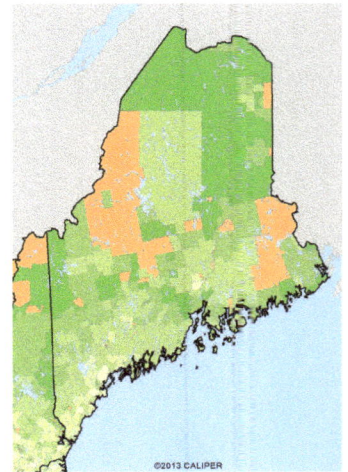

Based on the historical response in the long-term, average expenditures will increase to $1,136 or 2.20 percent of 2014 median household income − 1.21 percent in the upper-income parts of Cumberland County and 5.87 percent in the lower-income parts of Androscoggin County.

EXPENDITURES AS A PERCENTAGE OF MEDIAN HOUSEHOLD INCOME: LONG-TERM

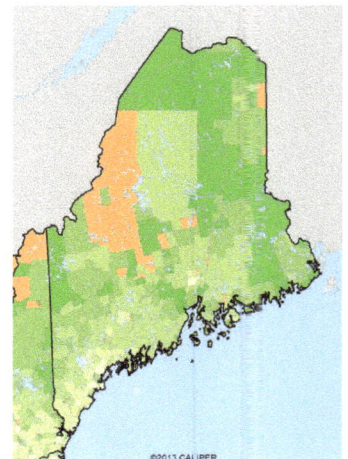

LEGEND

	0.9% and below
	0.9% to 1.4%
	1.4% to 1.8%
	1.8% to 2.2%
	2.2% to 2.6%
	2.6% to 3.0%
	3.0% to 5.0%
	5.0% to 7.5%
	7.5% to 10%
	10% and above
	Other

Maryland

As of 2014, the average annual expenditures on electricity in Maryland were $1,607, or 2.11 percent of the 2014 median household income of $76,165. The cost burden ranges from a low of 0.87 percent in parts of Montgomery County (median household income of at least $250,000), to a high of 14.46 percent in low-income parts of Baltimore County (median household income of $7,500).

2014 EXPENDITURES AS A PERCENTAGE OF MEDIAN HOUSEHOLD INCOME

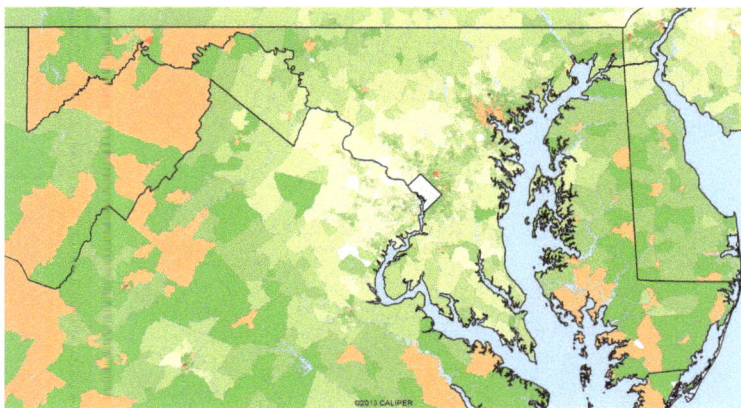

If the CPP is implemented, and consumers do not change their behavior, the cost burden will increase significantly to an average of $2,073 or 2.72 percent of 2014 median household income. In the high-income parts of Montgomery County, the burden increases to 1.12 percent, while in the low-income parts of Baltimore County the burden increases to 18.66 percent.

EXPENDITURES AS A PERCENTAGE OF MEDIAN HOUSEHOLD INCOME: STATIC ANALYSIS

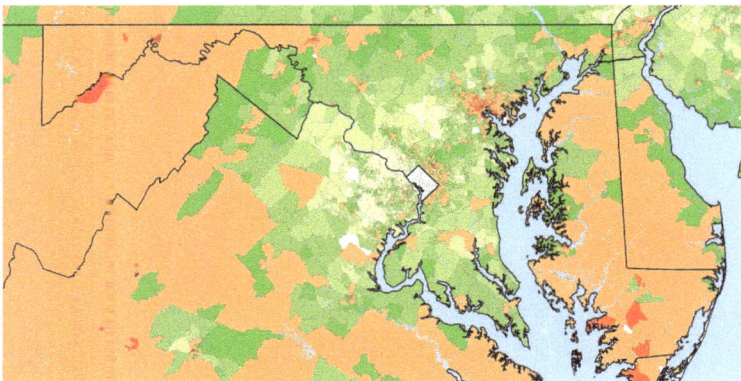

FACTS

- On average, Maryland residents could face annual electricity bills of $2,073 under the proposed Clean Power Plan.

- Low-income residents of Baltimore County could see average electricity expenditures rise to 18.66 percent of their annual income under the proposal.

- Calvert County residents could see their electricity costs rise by 22.6 percent annually, while City of Baltimore residents could see theirs rise by 22.5 percent.

LEGEND

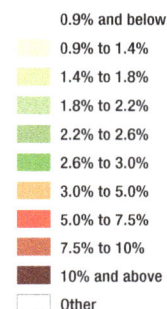

- 0.9% and below
- 0.9% to 1.4%
- 1.4% to 1.8%
- 1.8% to 2.2%
- 2.2% to 2.6%
- 2.6% to 3.0%
- 3.0% to 5.0%
- 5.0% to 7.5%
- 7.5% to 10%
- 10% and above
- Other

If consumers economize on their electricity consumption following the implementation of the CPP, the cost burden will increase but by less than under the static scenario. Based on the historical response in the short-term, average expenditures will increase to $1,924 or 2.53 percent of 2014 median household income − 1.04 percent in parts of Montgomery County and 17.32 percent in parts of Baltimore County.

EXPENDITURES AS A PERCENTAGE OF MEDIAN HOUSEHOLD INCOME SHORT-TERM

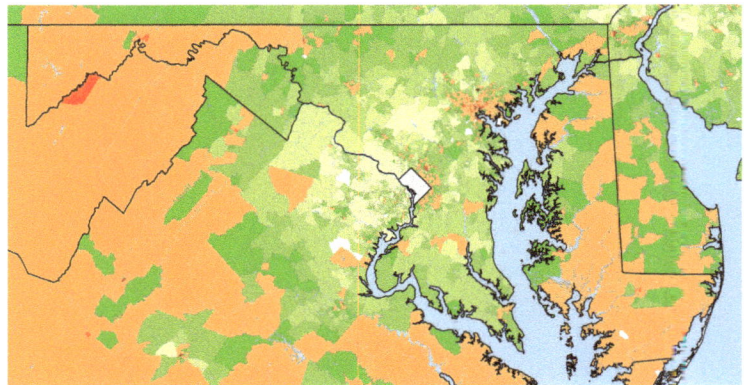

Based on the historical response in the long-term, average expenditures will increase to $1,909 or 2.51 percent of 2014 median household income − 1.04 percent in the upper-income parts of Montgomery County and 17.18 percent in the lower-income parts of Baltimore County.

EXPENDITURES AS A PERCENTAGE OF MEDIAN HOUSEHOLD INCOME LONG-TERM

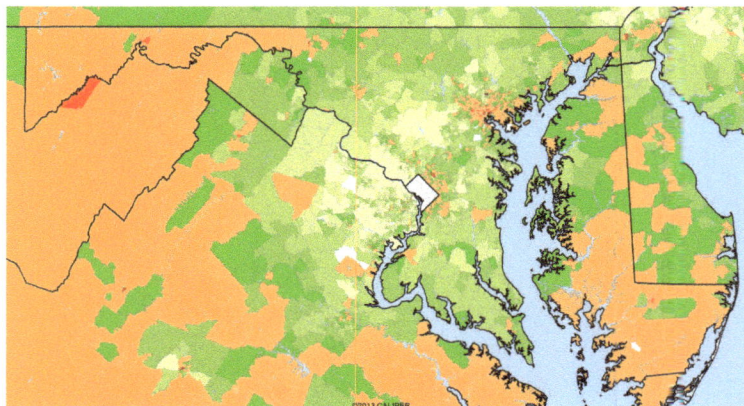

LEGEND

- 0.9% and below
- 0.9% to 1.4%
- 1.4% to 1.8%
- 1.8% to 2.2%
- 2.2% to 2.6%
- 2.6% to 3.0%
- 3.0% to 5.0%
- 5.0% to 7.5%
- 7.5% to 10%
- 10% and above
- Other

Massachusetts

As of 2014, the average annual expenditures on electricity in Massachusetts were $1,258, or 1.99 percent of the 2014 median household income of $63,151. The cost burden ranges from a low of 0.75 percent in parts of Middlesex County (median household income of $226,181), to a high of 14.56 percent in low-income parts of Hampshire County (median household income of $5,833).

2014 EXPENDITURES AS A PERCENTAGE OF MEDIAN HOUSEHOLD INCOME

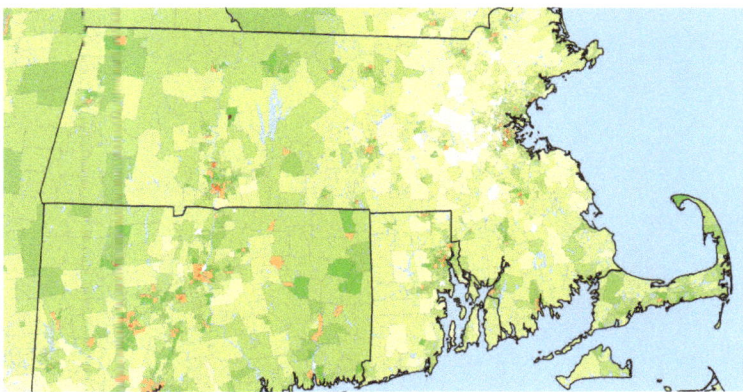

If the CPP is implemented, and consumers do not change their behavior, the cost burden will increase significantly to an average of $1,460 or 2.31 percent of 2014 median household income. In the high-income parts of Middlesex County, the burden increases to 0.87 percent, while in the low-income parts of Hampshire County the burden increases to 16.89 percent.

EXPENDITURES AS A PERCENTAGE OF MEDIAN HOUSEHOLD INCOME: STATIC ANALYSIS

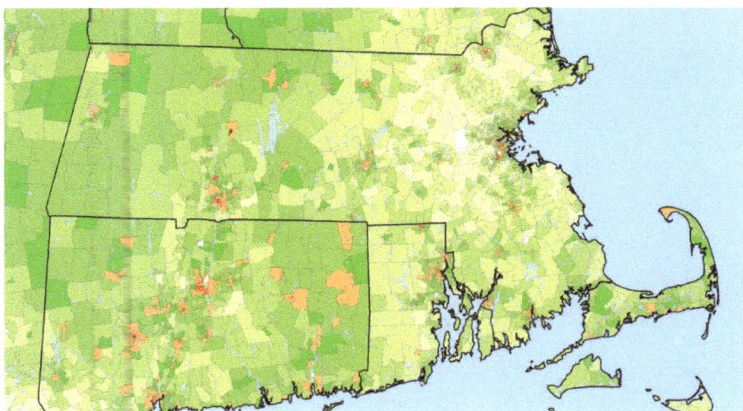

LEGEND

- 0.9% and below
- 0.9% to 1.4%
- 1.4% to 1.8%
- 1.8% to 2.2%
- 2.2% to 2.6%
- 2.6% to 3.0%
- 3.0% to 5.0%
- 5.0% to 7.5%
- 7.5% to 10%
- 10% and above
- Other

If consumers economize on their electricity consumption following the implementation of the CPP, the cost burden will increase but by less than under the static scenario. Based on the historical response in the short-term, average expenditures will increase to $1,421 or 2.25 percent of 2014 median household income – 0.85 percent in parts of Middlesex County and 16.45 percent in parts of Hampshire County.

EXPENDITURES AS A PERCENTAGE OF MEDIAN HOUSEHOLD INCOME: SHORT-TERM

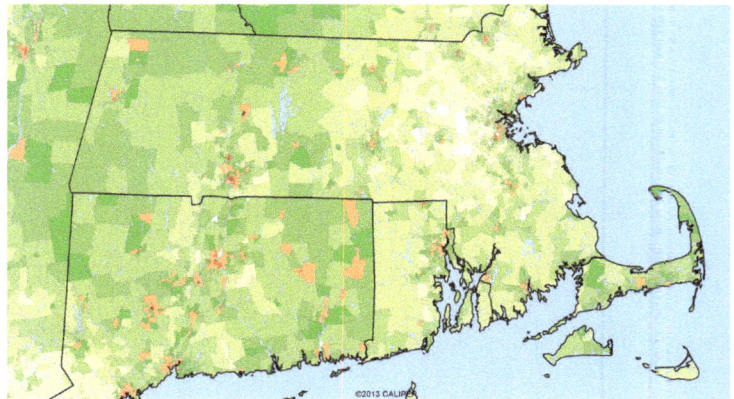

Based on the historical response in the long-term, average expenditures will increase to $1,394 or 2.21 percent of 2014 median household income – 0.83 percent in the upper-income parts of Middlesex County and 16.14 percent in the lower-income parts of Hampshire County.

EXPENDITURES AS A PERCENTAGE OF MEDIAN HOUSEHOLD INCOME: LONG-TERM

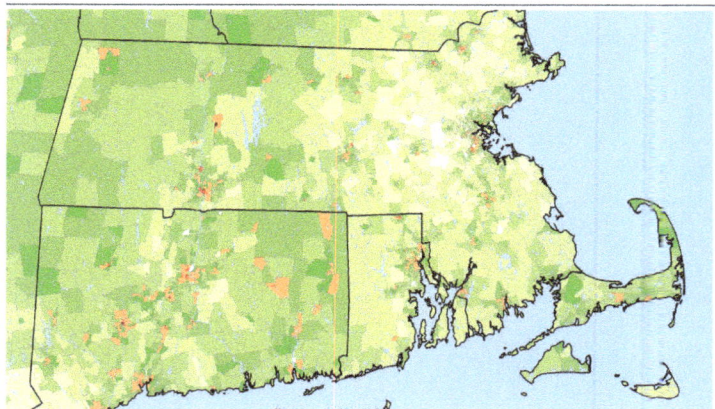

LEGEND

- 0.9% and below
- 0.9% to 1.4%
- 1.4% to 1.8%
- 1.8% to 2.2%
- 2.2% to 2.6%
- 2.6% to 3.0%
- 3.0% to 5.0%
- 5.0% to 7.5%
- 7.5% to 10%
- 10% and above
- Other

Michigan

As of 2014, the average annual expenditures on electricity in Michigan were $1,136, or 2.19 percent of the 2014 median household income of $52,005. The cost burden ranges from a low of 0.70 percent in parts of Wayne County (median household income of $180,125), to a high of 8.93 percent in low-income parts of Marquette County (median household income of $8,594).

2014 EXPENDITURES AS A PERCENTAGE OF MEDIAN HOUSEHOLD INCOME

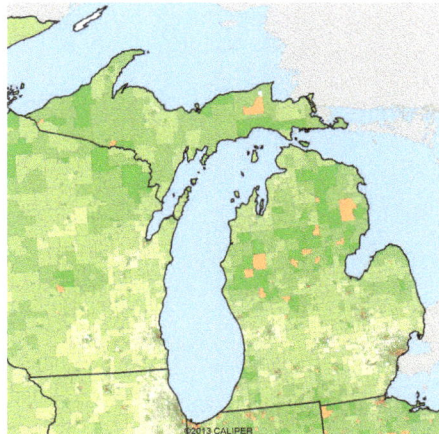

If the CPP is implemented, and consumers do not change their behavior, the cost burden will increase significantly to an average of $1,448 or 2.78 percent of 2014 median household income. In the high-income parts of Wayne County, the burden increases to 0.89 percent, while in the low-income parts of Marquette County the burden increases to 11.37 percent.

EXPENDITURES AS A PERCENTAGE OF MEDIAN HOUSEHOLD INCOME: STATIC ANALYSIS

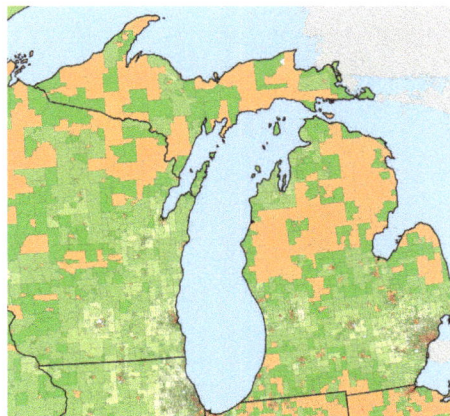

LEGEND

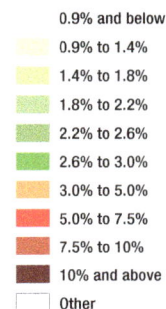

0.9% and below
0.9% to 1.4%
1.4% to 1.8%
1.8% to 2.2%
2.2% to 2.6%
2.6% to 3.0%
3.0% to 5.0%
5.0% to 7.5%
7.5% to 10%
10% and above
Other

If consumers economize on their electricity consumption following the implementation of the CPP, the cost burden will increase but by less than under the static scenario. Based on the historical response in the short-term, average expenditures will increase to $1,397 or 2.69 percent of 2014 median household income – 0.86 percent in parts of Wayne County and 10.97 percent in parts of Marquette County.

EXPENDITURES AS A
PERCENTAGE OF MEDIAN
HOUSEHOLD INCOME:
SHORT-TERM

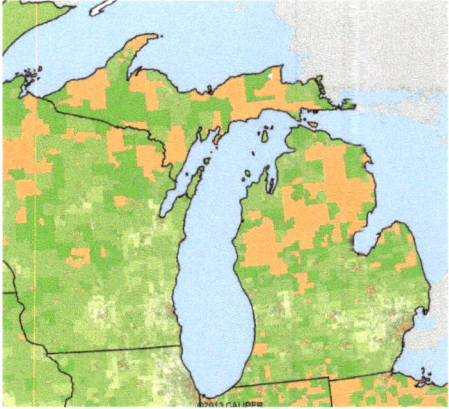

Based on the historical response in the long-term, average expenditures will increase to $1,372 or 2.64 percent of 2014 median household income – 0.84 percent in the upper-income parts of Wayne County and 10.78 percent in the lower-income parts of Marquette County.

EXPENDITURES AS A
PERCENTAGE OF MEDIAN
HOUSEHOLD INCOME:
LONG-TERM

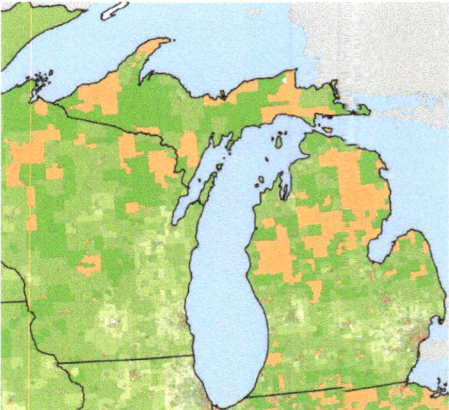

LEGEND

- 0.9% and below
- 0.9% to 1.4%
- 1.4% to 1.8%
- 1.8% to 2.2%
- 2.2% to 2.6%
- 2.6% to 3.0%
- 3.0% to 5.0%
- 5.0% to 7.5%
- 7.5% to 10%
- 10% and above
- Other

Minnesota

As of 2014, the average annual expenditures on electricity in Minnesota were $1,170, or 1.74 percent of the 2014 median household income of $67,244. The cost burden ranges from a low of 0.73 percent in parts of Hennepin County (median household income of $177,727), to a high of 6.45 percent in low-income parts of Hennepin County (median household income of $12,255).

2014 EXPENDITURES AS A
PERCENTAGE OF MEDIAN
HOUSEHOLD INCOME

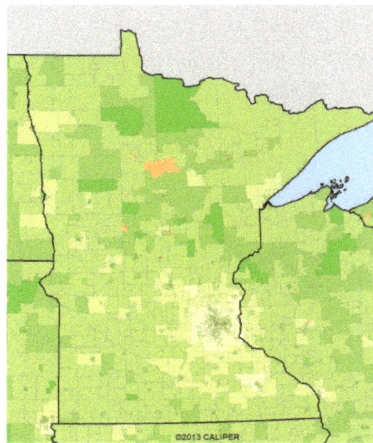

If the CPP is implemented, and consumers do not change their behavior, the cost burden will increase significantly to an average of $1,463 or 2.18 percent of 2014 median household income. In the high-income parts of Hennepin County, the burden increases to 0.91 percent, while in the low-income parts of Hennepin County the burden increases to 8.06 percent.

EXPENDITURES AS A PERCENTAGE
OF MEDIAN HOUSEHOLD INCOME:
STATIC ANALYSIS

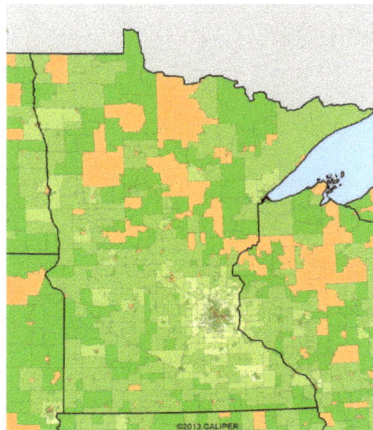

FACTS

- Minnesota residents could soon face annual electricity costs of $1,463 on average under the proposed Clean Power Plan.

- Poor residents of Hennepin County could see average annual electricity expenditures rise to 8.06 percent of their income if the plan takes effect.

- Wadena County residents could see their power bills rise by 20.1 percent annually, while Koochiching County residents could see theirs rise by 20.0 percent.

LEGEND

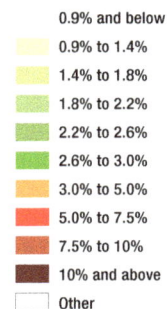

0.9% and below
0.9% to 1.4%
1.4% to 1.8%
1.8% to 2.2%
2.2% to 2.6%
2.6% to 3.0%
3.0% to 5.0%
5.0% to 7.5%
7.5% to 10%
10% and above
Other

If consumers economize on their electricity consumption following the implementation of the CPP, the cost burden will increase but by less than under the static scenario. Based on the historical response in the short-term, average expenditures will increase to $1,415 or 2.10 percent of 2014 median household income – 0.88 percent in parts of Hennepin County and 7.80 percent in the low-income parts of Hennepin County.

EXPENDITURES AS A PERCENTAGE
OF MEDIAN HOUSEHOLD INCOME:
SHORT-TERM

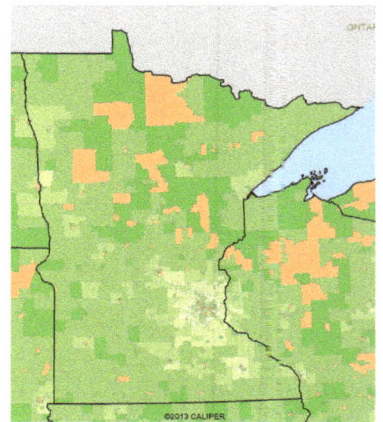

Based on the historical response in the long-term, average expenditures will increase to $1,391 or 2.07 percent of 2014 median household income – 0.87 percent in the upper-income parts of Hennepin County and 7.66 percent in the lower-income parts of Hennepin County.

EXPENDITURES AS A PERCENTAGE
OF MEDIAN HOUSEHOLD INCOME:
LONG-TERM

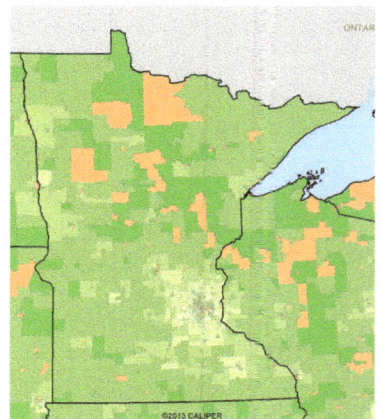

LEGEND

	0.9% and below
	0.9% to 1.4%
	1.4% to 1.8%
	1.8% to 2.2%
	2.2% to 2.6%
	2.6% to 3.0%
	3.0% to 5.0%
	5.0% to 7.5%
	7.5% to 10%
	10% and above
	Other

Mississippi

As of 2014, the average annual expenditures on electricity in Mississippi were $1,697, or 4.78 percent of the 2014 median household income of $35,521. The cost burden ranges from a low of 1.51 percent in parts of Madison County (median household income of $124,477), to a high of 9.84 percent in low-income parts of Harrison County (median household income of $11,638).

2014 EXPENDITURES AS A PERCENTAGE OF MEDIAN HOUSEHOLD INCOME

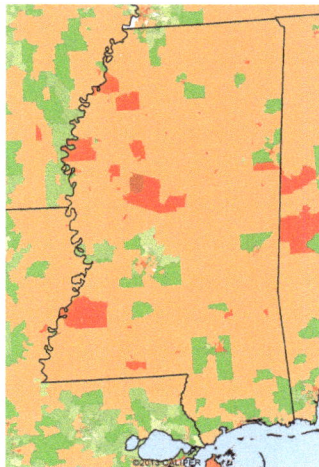

If the CPP is implemented, and consumers do not change their behavior, the cost burden will increase significantly to an average of $2,079 or 5.85 percent of 2014 median household income. In the high-income parts of Madison County, the burden increases to 1.85 percent, while in the low-income parts of Harrison County the burden increases to 12.06 percent.

EXPENDITURES AS A PERCENTAGE OF MEDIAN HOUSEHOLD INCOME: STATIC ANALYSIS

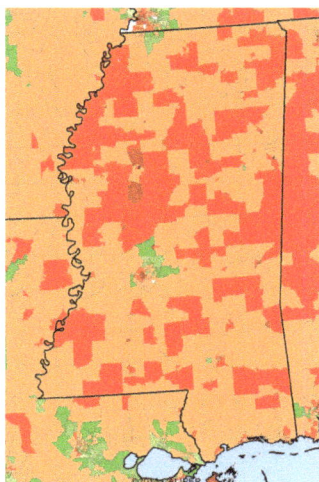

FACTS

- Mississippi households could soon be paying nearly $2,100 a year on average for electricity under the Obama Clean Power Plan.

- In the poorest communities in Harrison County, residents could see average electricity expenditures rise to more than 12 percent of their annual income if the plan is implemented.

- Walthall County residents could see their annual power costs rise 18.5 percent, while Yazoo County residents could see theirs go up by 18.4 percent.

LEGEND

- 0.9% and below
- 0.9% to 1.4%
- 1.4% to 1.8%
- 1.8% to 2.2%
- 2.2% to 2.6%
- 2.6% to 3.0%
- 3.0% to 5.0%
- 5.0% to 7.5%
- 7.5% to 10%
- 10% and above
- Other

If consumers economize on their electricity consumption following the implementation of the CPP, the cost burden will increase but by less than under the static scenario. Based on the historical response in the short-term, average expenditures will increase to $1,977 or 5.57 percent of 2014 median household income – 1.76 percent in parts of Madison County and 11.47 percent in the low-income parts of Harrison County.

EXPENDITURES AS A PERCENTAGE OF
MEDIAN HOUSEHOLD INCOME:
SHORT-TERM

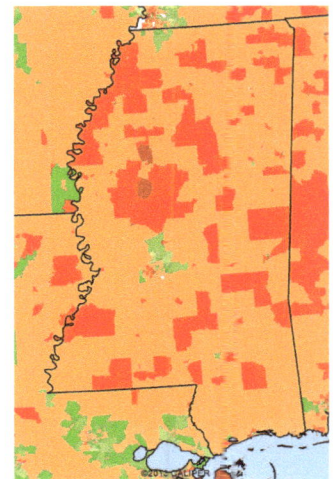

Based on the historical response in the long-term, average expenditures will increase to $1,843 or 5.19 percent of 2014 median household income – 1.64 percent in the upper-income parts of Madison County and 10.69 percent in the lower-income parts of Harrison County.

EXPENDITURES AS A PERCENTAGE OF
MEDIAN HOUSEHOLD INCOME:
LONG-TERM

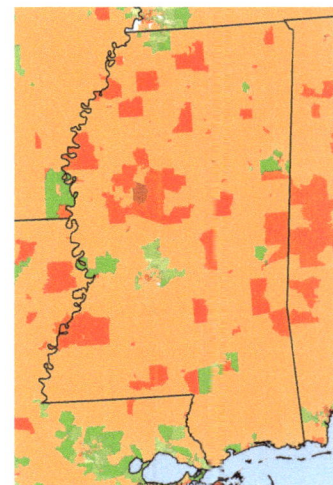

LEGEND

	0.9% and below
	0.9% to 1.4%
	1.4% to 1.8%
	1.8% to 2.2%
	2.2% to 2.6%
	2.6% to 3.0%
	3.0% to 5.0%
	5.0% to 7.5%
	7.5% to 10%
	10% and above
	Other

Missouri

As of 2014, the average annual expenditures on electricity in Missouri were $1,399, or 2.47 percent of the 2014 median household income of $56,630. The cost burden ranges from a low of 0.82 percent in parts of St. Louis County (median household income of $200,000), to a high of 14.12 percent in low-income parts of Greene County (median household income of $6,689).

2014 EXPENDITURES AS A
PERCENTAGE OF MEDIAN
HOUSEHOLD INCOME

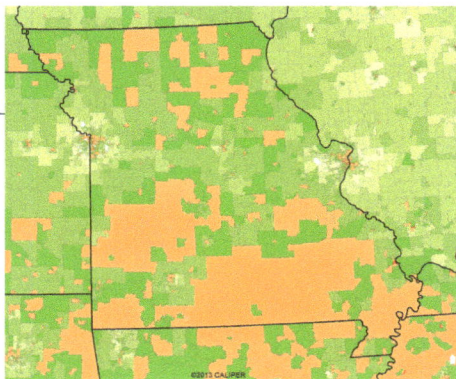

If the CPP is implemented, and consumers do not change their behavior, the cost burden will increase significantly to an average of $1,767 or 3.12 percent of 2014 median household income. In the high-income parts of St. Louis County, the burden increases to 1.04 percent, while in the low-income parts of Greene County the burden increases to 17.84 percent.

EXPENDITURES AS A
PERCENTAGE OF MEDIAN
HOUSEHOLD INCOME:
STATIC ANALYSIS

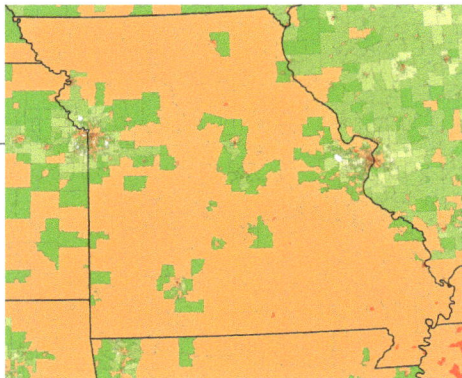

"In Missouri, about half of the state's households already spend 18 cents of every take-home dollar on energy. My constituents tell me that they cannot afford to pay higher utility bills."

—Missouri State Rep. Jack Rondon

FACT

Missouri families could soon be paying $1,767 annual power bill on average if the Obama Clean Power Plan is implemented.

LEGEND

- 0.9% and below
- 0.9% to 1.4%
- 1.4% to 1.8%
- 1.8% to 2.2%
- 2.2% to 2.6%
- 2.6% to 3.0%
- 3.0% to 5.0%
- 5.0% to 7.5%
- 7.5% to 10%
- 10% and above
- Other

If consumers economize on their electricity consumption following the implementation of the CPP, the cost burden will increase but by less than under the static scenario. Based on the historical response in the short-term, average expenditures will increase to $1,707 or 3.01 percent of 2014 median household income – 1.00 percent in parts of St. Louis County and 17.23 percent in the low-income parts of Greene County.

EXPENDITURES AS A
PERCENTAGE OF MEDIAN
HOUSEHOLD INCOME:
SHORT-TERM

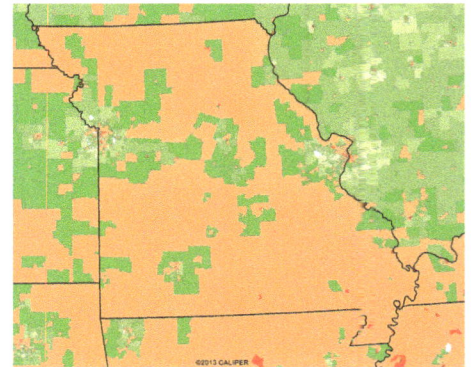

Based on the historical response in the long-term, average expenditures will increase to $1,677 or 2.96 percent of 2014 median household income – 0.99 percent in the upper-income parts of St. Louis County and 16.93 percent in the lower-income parts of Greene County.

EXPENDITURES AS A
PERCENTAGE OF MEDIAN
HOUSEHOLD INCOME:
LONG-TERM

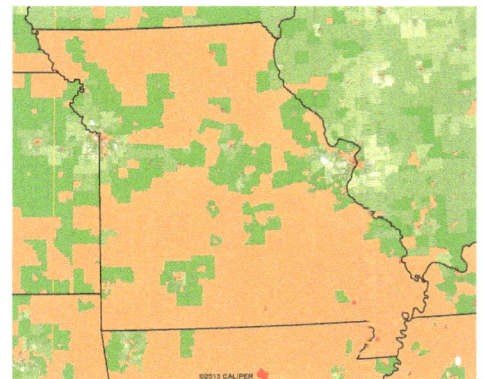

LEGEND

- 0.9% and below
- 0.9% to 1.4%
- 1.4% to 1.8%
- 1.8% to 2.2%
- 2.2% to 2.6%
- 2.6% to 3.0%
- 3.0% to 5.0%
- 5.0% to 7.5%
- 7.5% to 10%
- 10% and above
- Other

Montana

As of 2014, the average annual expenditures on electricity in Montana were $1,037, or 2.03 percent of the 2014 median household income of $51,102. The cost burden ranges from a low of 1.00 percent in parts of Yellowstone County (median household income of $115,000), to a high of 5.14 percent in low-income parts of Gallatin County (median household income of $13,622).

2014 EXPENDITURES AS A PERCENTAGE OF MEDIAN HOUSEHOLD INCOME

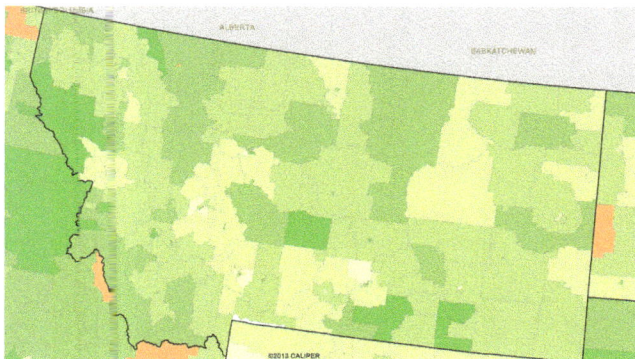

If the CPP is implemented, and consumers do not change their behavior, the cost burden will increase significantly to an average of $1,196 or 2.34 percent of 2014 median household income. In the high-income parts of Yellowstone County, the burden increases to 1.15 percent, while in the low-income parts of Gallatin County the burden increases to 5.93 percent.

EXPENDITURES AS A PERCENTAGE OF MEDIAN HOUSEHOLD INCOME: STATIC ANALYSIS

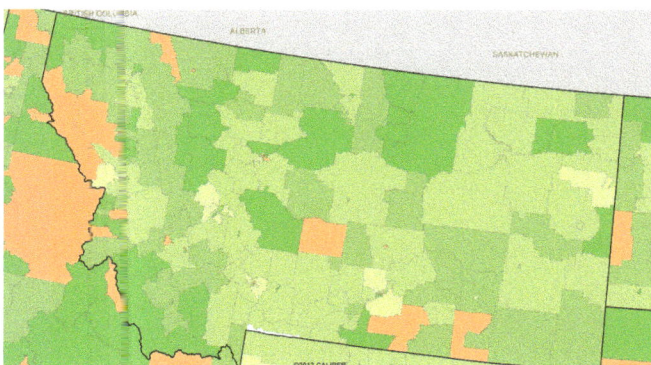

FACTS

- Montana residents could soon be paying $1,154 annually for electricity under the Obama climate agenda.

- The University of Montana Bureau of Business and Economic Research has found that the Clean Power Plan could result in 7,100 lost jobs in Montana and $500 million in lost annual income.

- Montana residents could soon be paying nearly $1,200 a year for electricity on average under the Obama Clean Power Plan.

LEGEND

- 0.9% and below
- 0.9% to 1.4%
- 1.4% to 1.8%
- 1.8% to 2.2%
- 2.2% to 2.6%
- 2.6% to 3.0%
- 3.0% to 5.0%
- 5.0% to 7.5%
- 7.5% to 10%
- 10% and above
- Other

If consumers economize on their electricity consumption following the implementation of the CPP, the cost burden will increase but by less than under the static scenario. Based on the historical response in the short-term, average expenditures will increase to $1,163 or 2.28 percent of 2014 median household income – 1.12 percent in parts of Yellowstone County and 5.76 percent in the low-income parts of Gallatin County.

EXPENDITURES AS A PERCENTAGE OF MEDIAN HOUSEHOLD INCOME: SHORT-TERM

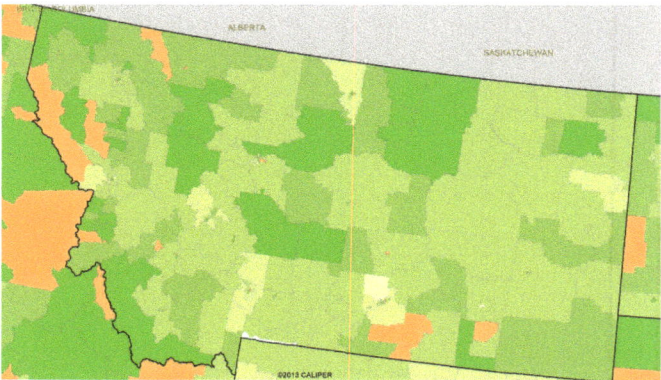

Based on the historical response in the long-term, average expenditures will increase to $1,154 or 2.26 percent of 2014 median household income – 1.11 percent in the upper-income parts of Yellowstone County and 5.72 percent in the lower-income parts of Gallatin County.

EXPENDITURES AS A PERCENTAGE OF MEDIAN HOUSEHOLD INCOME: LONG-TERM

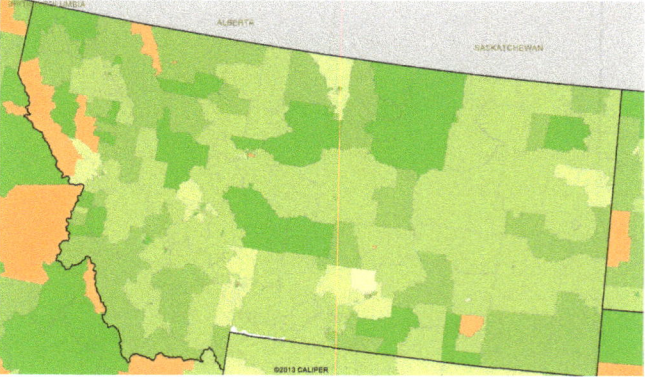

LEGEND

- 0.9% and below
- 0.9% to 1.4%
- 1.4% to 1.8%
- 1.8% to 2.2%
- 2.2% to 2.6%
- 2.6% to 3.0%
- 3.0% to 5.0%
- 5.0% to 7.5%
- 7.5% to 10%
- 10% and above
- Other

Nebraska

As of 2014, the average annual expenditures on electricity in Nebraska were $1,278, or 2.25 percent of the 2014 median household income of $56,870. The cost burden ranges from a low of 0.74 percent in parts of Douglas County (median household income of $190,789), to a high of 12.94 percent in low-income parts of Lancaster County (median household income of $6,667).

2014 EXPENDITURES AS A PERCENTAGE OF MEDIAN HOUSEHOLD INCOME

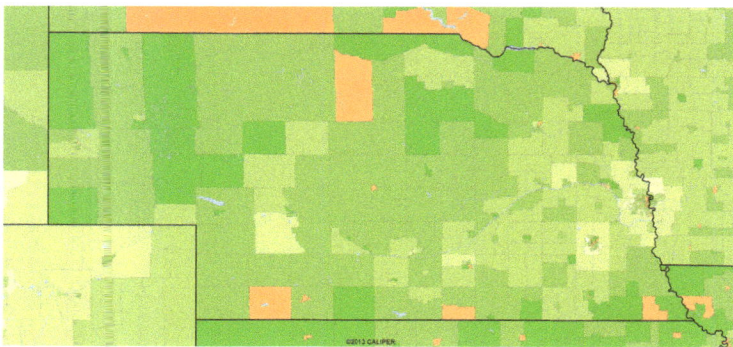

If the CPP is implemented, and consumers do not change their behavior, the cost burden will increase significantly to an average of $1,579 or 2.78 percent of 2014 median household income. In the high-income parts of Douglas County, the burden increases to 0.92 percent, while in the low-income parts of Lancaster County the burden increases to 15.99 percent.

EXPENDITURES AS A PERCENTAGE OF MEDIAN HOUSEHOLD INCOME: STATIC ANALYSIS

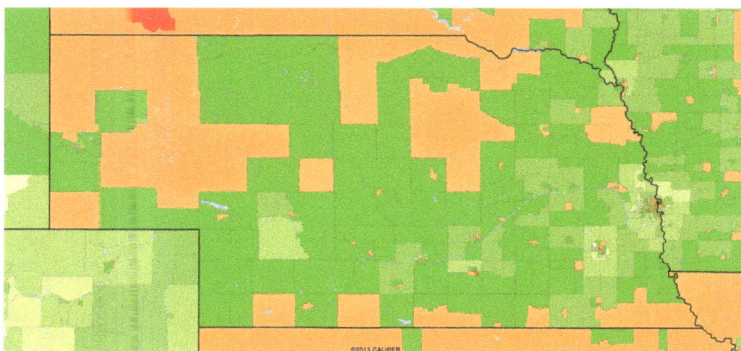

"Left unchecked, this inappropriate jurisdictional overreach of the federal government will have serious consequences by driving electrical costs up for all Nebraskans across our state."

—State Attorney General Doug Peterson

FACT

Nebraska families could soon be paying nearly $1,600 annually on average for electricity under the Obama climate agenda.

LEGEND

- 0.9% and below
- 0.9% to 1.4%
- 1.4% to 1.8%
- 1.8% to 2.2%
- 2.2% to 2.6%
- 2.6% to 3.0%
- 3.0% to 5.0%
- 5.0% to 7.5%
- 7.5% to 10%
- 10% and above
- Other

If consumers economize on their electricity consumption following the implementation of the CPP, the cost burden will increase but by less than under the static scenario. Based on the historical response in the short-term, average expenditures will increase to $1,530 or 2.69 percent of 2014 median household income – 0.89 percent in parts of Douglas County and 15.49 percent in the low-income parts of Lancaster County.

EXPENDITURES AS A PERCENTAGE OF MEDIAN HOUSEHOLD INCOME: SHORT-TERM

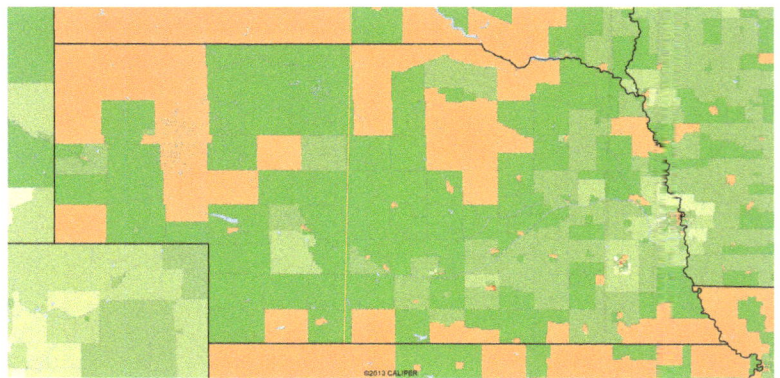

Based on the historical response in the long-term, average expenditures will increase to $1,505 or 2.65 percent of 2014 median household income – 0.87 percent in the upper-income parts of Douglas County and 15.24 percent in the lower-income parts of Lancaster County.

EXPENDITURES AS A PERCENTAGE OF MEDIAN HOUSEHOLD INCOME: LONG-TERM

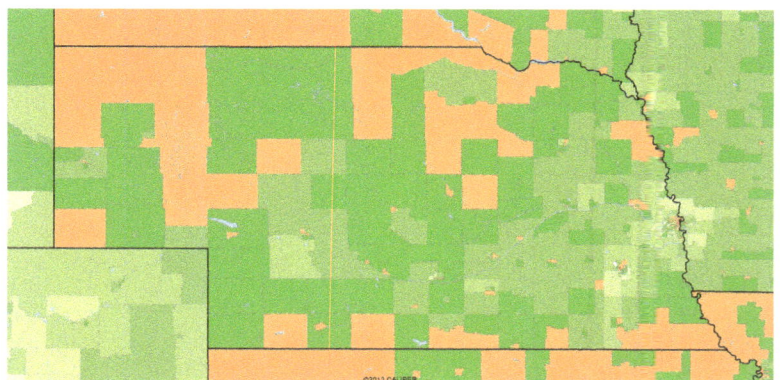

LEGEND

- 0.9% and below
- 0.9% to 1.4%
- 1.4% to 1.8%
- 1.8% to 2.2%
- 2.2% to 2.6%
- 2.6% to 3.0%
- 3.0% to 5.0%
- 5.0% to 7.5%
- 7.5% to 10%
- 10% and above
- Other

Nevada

As of 2014, the average annual expenditures on electricity in Nevada were $1,389 or 2.79 percent of the 2014 median household income of $49,875. The cost burden ranges from a low of 1.00 percent in parts of Clark County (median household income of $153,133), to a high of 6.47 percent in low-income parts of Washoe County (median household income of $14,488).

2014 EXPENDITURES AS A
PERCENTAGE OF MEDIAN
HOUSEHOLD INCOME

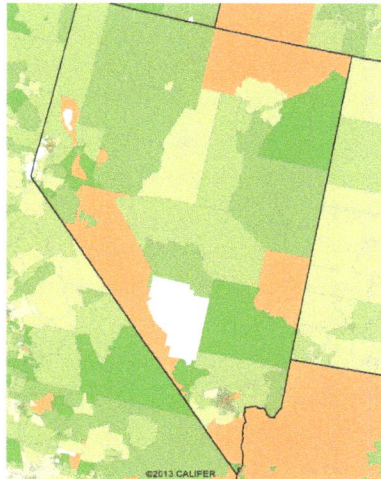

If the CPP is implemented, and consumers do not change their behavior, the cost burden will increase significantly to an average of $1,573 or 3.15 percent of 2014 median household income. In the high-income parts of Clark County, the burden increases to 1.14 percent, while in the low-income parts of Washoe County the burden increases to 7.33 percent.

EXPENDITURES AS A
PERCENTAGE OF MEDIAN
HOUSEHOLD INCOME: STATIC
ANALYSIS

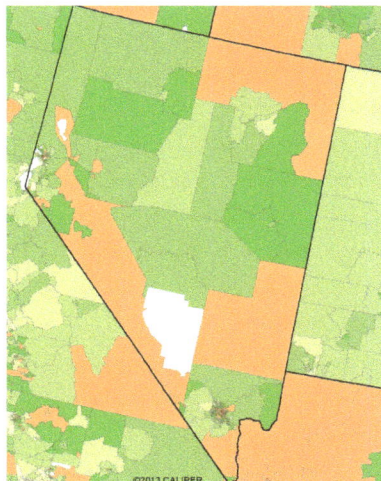

LEGEND

	0.9% and below
	0.9% to 1.4%
	1.4% to 1.8%
	1.8% to 2.2%
	2.2% to 2.6%
	2.6% to 3.0%
	3.0% to 5.0%
	5.0% to 7.5%
	7.5% to 10%
	10% and above
	Other

If consumers economize on their electricity consumption following the implementation of the CPP, the cost burden will increase but by less than under the static scenario. Based on the historical response in the short-term, average expenditures will increase to $1,534 or 3.08 percent of 2014 median household income – 1.11 percent in parts of Clark County and 7.15 percent in the low-income parts of Washoe County.

EXPENDITURES AS A PERCENTAGE
OF MEDIAN HOUSEHOLD INCOME:
SHORT-TERM

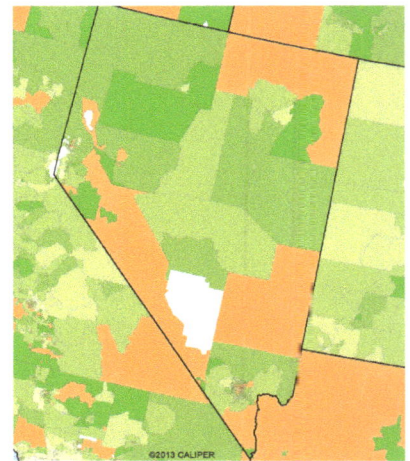

Based on the historical response in the long-term, average expenditures will increase to $1,524 or 3.06 percent of 2014 median household income – 1.10 percent in the upper-income parts of Clark County and 7.10 percent in the lower-income parts of Washoe County.

EXPENDITURES AS A PERCENTAGE
OF MEDIAN HOUSEHOLD INCOME:
LONG-TERM

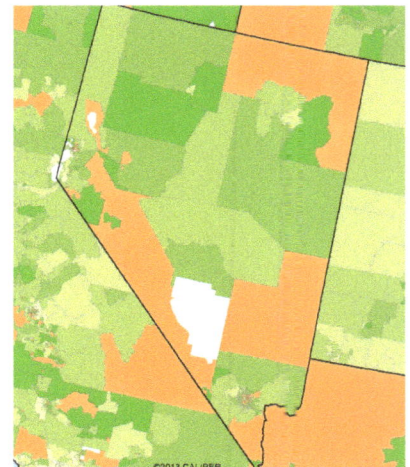

LEGEND

	0.9% and below
	0.9% to 1.4%
	1.4% to 1.8%
	1.8% to 2.2%
	2.2% to 2.6%
	2.6% to 3.0%
	3.0% to 5.0%
	5.0% to 7.5%
	7.5% to 10%
	10% and above
	Other

New Hampshire

As of 2014, the average annual expenditures on electricity in New Hampshire were $1,296 or 1.77 percent of the 2014 median household income of $73,397. The cost burden ranges from a low of 0.86 percent in parts of Hillsborough County (median household income of $166,324), to a high of 4.11 percent in low-income parts of Hillsborough County (median household income of $21,265).

2014 EXPENDITURES AS A PERCENTAGE OF MEDIAN HOUSEHOLD INCOME

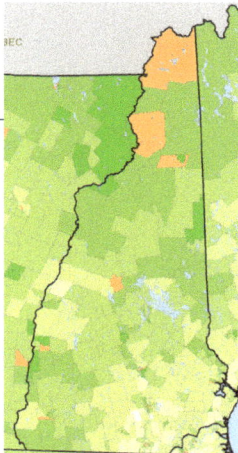

If the CPP is implemented, and consumers do not change their behavior, the cost burden will increase significantly to an average of $1,484 or 2.02 percent of 2014 median household income. In the high-income parts of Hillsborough County, the burden increases to 0.99 percent, while in the low-income parts of Hillsborough County the burden increases to 4.71 percent.

EXPENDITURES AS A PERCENTAGE OF MEDIAN HOUSEHOLD INCOME: STATIC ANALYSIS

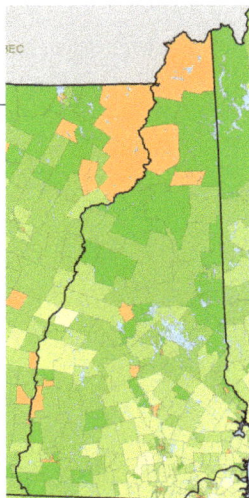

LEGEND

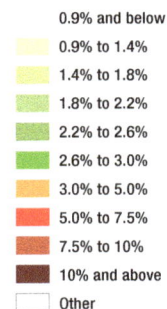

- 0.9% and below
- 0.9% to 1.4%
- 1.4% to 1.8%
- 1.8% to 2.2%
- 2.2% to 2.6%
- 2.6% to 3.0%
- 3.0% to 5.0%
- 5.0% to 7.5%
- 7.5% to 10%
- 10% and above
- Other

If consumers economize on their electricity consumption following the implementation of the CPP, the cost burden will increase but by less than under the static scenario. Based on the historical response in the short-term, average expenditures will increase to $1,448 or 1.97 percent of 2014 median household income – 0.96 percent in parts of Hillsborough County and 4.60 percent in the low-income parts of Hillsborough County.

EXPENDITURES AS A PERCENTAGE OF MEDIAN HOUSEHOLD INCOME: SHORT-TERM

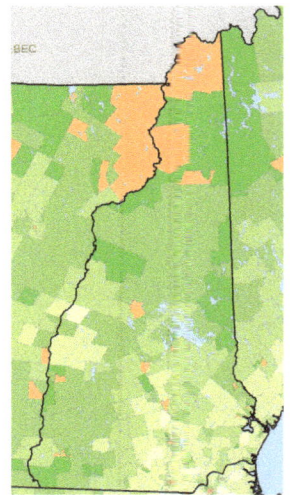

Based on the historical response in the long-term, average expenditures will increase to $1,423 or 1.94 percent of 2014 median household income – 0.95 percent in the upper-income parts of Hillsborough County and 4.52 percent in the lower-income parts of Hillsborough County.

EXPENDITURES AS A PERCENTAGE OF MEDIAN HOUSEHOLD INCOME: LONG-TERM

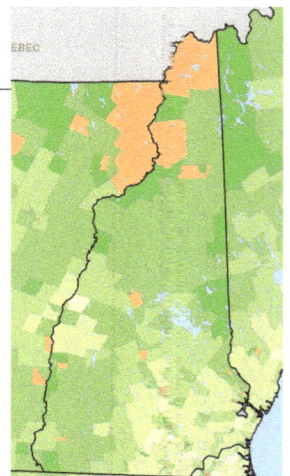

LEGEND

	0.9% and below
	0.9% to 1.4%
	1.4% to 1.8%
	1.8% to 2.2%
	2.2% to 2.6%
	2.6% to 3.0%
	3.0% to 5.0%
	5.0% to 7.5%
	7.5% to 10%
	10% and above
	Other

New Jersey

As of 2014, the average annual expenditures on electricity in New Jersey were $1,201 or 1.84 percent of the 2014 median household income of $65,243. The cost burden ranges from a low of 0.65 percent in parts of Bergen County (median household income of at least $250,000), to a high of 7.00 percent in low-income parts of Essex County (median household income of $11,594).

2014 EXPENDITURES AS A PERCENTAGE OF MEDIAN HOUSEHOLD INCOME

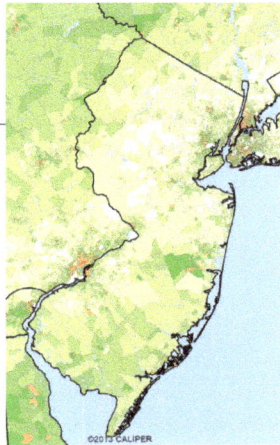

If the CPP is implemented, and consumers do not change their behavior, the cost burden will increase significantly to an average of $1,486 or 2.28 percent of 2014 median household income. In the high-income parts of Bergen County, the burden increases to 0.81 percent, while in the low-income parts of Essex County the burden increases to 8.65 percent.

EXPENDITURES AS A PERCENTAGE OF MEDIAN HOUSEHOLD INCOME: STATIC ANALYSIS

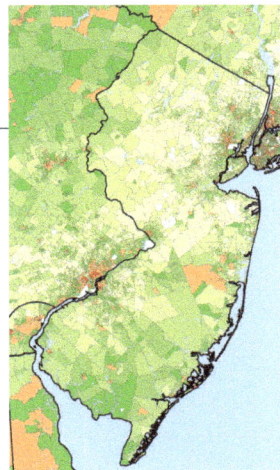

LEGEND

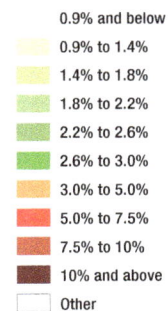

- 0.9% and below
- 0.9% to 1.4%
- 1.4% to 1.8%
- 1.8% to 2.2%
- 2.2% to 2.6%
- 2.6% to 3.0%
- 3.0% to 5.0%
- 5.0% to 7.5%
- 7.5% to 10%
- 10% and above
- Other

If consumers economize on their electricity consumption following the implementation of the CPP, the cost burden will increase but by less than under the static scenario. Based on the historical response in the short-term, average expenditures will increase to $1,431 or 2.19 percent of 2014 median household income − 0.78 percent in parts of Bergen County and 8.33 percent in the low-income parts of Essex County.

EXPENDITURES AS A PERCENTAGE OF
MEDIAN HOUSEHOLD INCOME:
SHORT-TERM

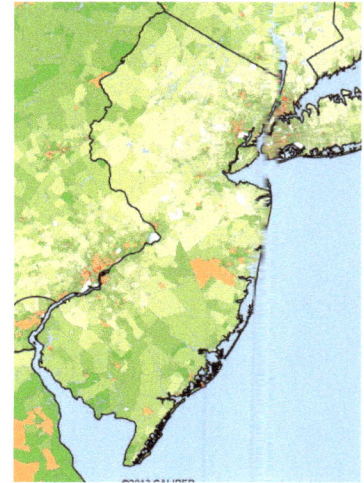

Based on the historical response in the long-term, average expenditures will increase to $1,393 or 2.14 percent of 2014 median household income − 0.76 percent in the upper-income parts of Bergen County and 8.11 percent in the lower-income parts of Essex County.

EXPENDITURES AS A PERCENTAGE OF
MEDIAN HOUSEHOLD INCOME:
LONG-TERM

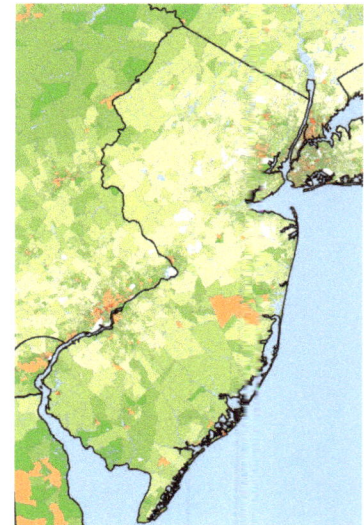

LEGEND

- 0.9% and below
- 0.9% to 1.4%
- 1.4% to 1.8%
- 1.8% to 2.2%
- 2.2% to 2.6%
- 2.6% to 3.0%
- 3.0% to 5.0%
- 5.0% to 7.5%
- 7.5% to 10%
- 10% and above
- Other

New Mexico

As of 2014, the average annual expenditures on electricity in New Mexico were $935 or 2.00 percent of the 2014 median household income of $46,686. The cost burden ranges from a low of 0.71 percent in parts of Santa Fe County (median household income of $145,156), to a high of 5.30 percent in low-income parts of Doña Ana County (median household income of $11,903).

2014 EXPENDITURES AS A PERCENTAGE OF MEDIAN HOUSEHOLD INCOME

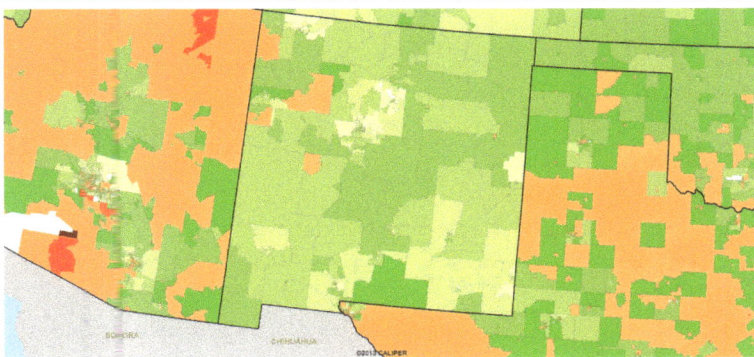

If the CPP is implemented, and consumers do not change their behavior, the cost burden will increase significantly to an average of $1,028 or 2.20 percent of 2014 median household income. In the high-income parts of Santa Fe County, the burden increases to 0.78 percent, while in the low-income parts of Doña Ana County the burden increases to 5.83 percent.

EXPENDITURES AS A PERCENTAGE OF MEDIAN HOUSEHOLD INCOME: STATIC ANALYSIS

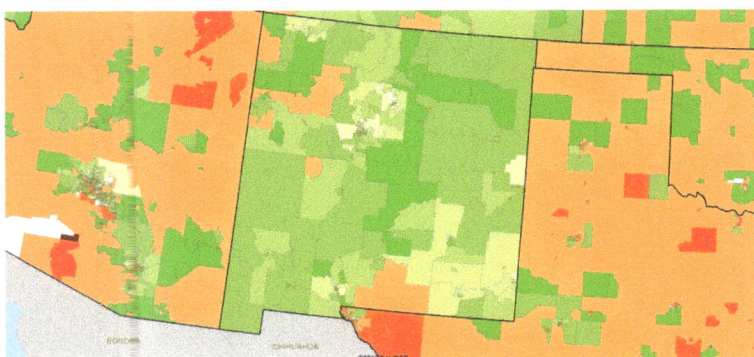

LEGEND

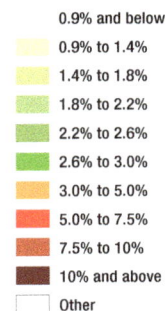

0.9% and below
0.9% to 1.4%
1.4% to 1.8%
1.8% to 2.2%
2.2% to 2.6%
2.6% to 3.0%
3.0% to 5.0%
5.0% to 7.5%
7.5% to 10%
10% and above
Other

If consumers economize on their electricity consumption following the implementation of the CPP, the cost burden will increase but by less than under the static scenario. Based on the historical response in the short-term, average expenditures will increase to $1,008 or 2.16 percent of 2014 median household income – 0.77 percent in parts of Santa Fe County and 5.72 percent in the low-income parts of Doña Ana County.

EXPENDITURES AS A PERCENTAGE OF MEDIAN HOUSEHOLD INCOME: SHORT-TERM

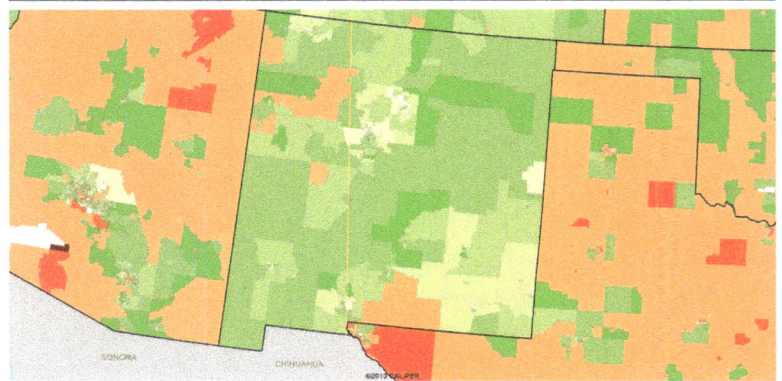

Based on the historical response in the long-term, average expenditures will increase to $1,003 or 2.15 percent of 2014 median household income – 0.77 percent in the upper-income parts of Santa Fe County and 5.69 percent in the lower-income parts of Doña Ana County.

EXPENDITURES AS A PERCENTAGE OF MEDIAN HOUSEHOLD INCOME: LONG-TERM

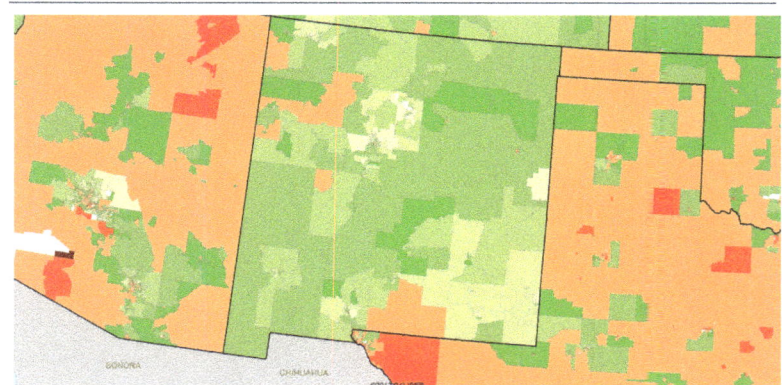

LEGEND

- 0.9% and below
- 0.9% to 1.4%
- 1.4% to 1.8%
- 1.8% to 2.2%
- 2.2% to 2.6%
- 2.6% to 3.0%
- 3.0% to 5.0%
- 5.0% to 7.5%
- 7.5% to 10%
- 10% and above
- Other

New York

As of 2014, the average annual expenditures on electricity in New York were $1,389 or 2.56 percent of the 2014 median household income of $54,310. The cost burden ranges from a low of 0.75 percent in parts of Richmond County (median household income of at least $250,000), to a high of 10.23 percent in low-income parts of Onondaga County (median household income of $9,171).

2014 EXPENDITURES AS A PERCENTAGE OF MEDIAN HOUSEHOLD INCOME

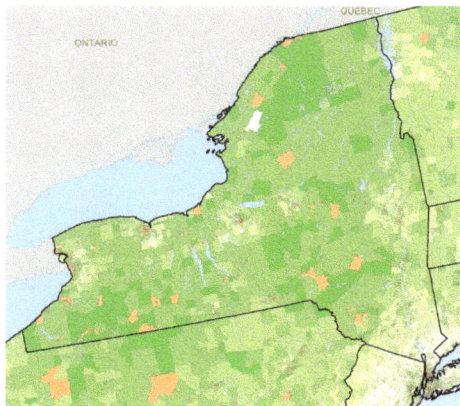

If the CPP is implemented, and consumers do not change their behavior, the cost burden will increase significantly to an average of $1,634 or 3.01 percent of 2014 median household income. In the high-income parts of Richmond County, the burden increases to 0.89 percent, while in the low-income parts of Onondaga County the burden increases to 12.03 percent.

EXPENDITURES AS A PERCENTAGE OF MEDIAN HOUSEHOLD INCOME: STATIC ANALYSIS

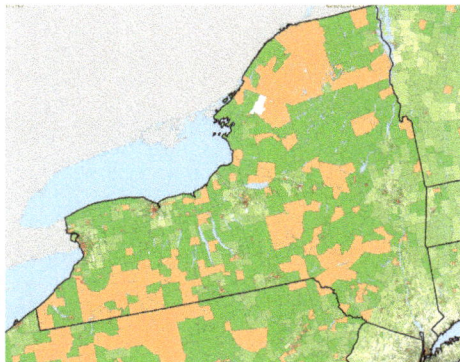

FACTS

- New York residents could face average annual electricity bills of $1,634 under the Clean Power Plan.

- Residents in low-income areas of Onondaga County could see average electricity expenditures increase to more than 12 percent of their annual income.

- Bronx and Rockland County residents could see annual power costs rise by 15.1 percent.

LEGEND

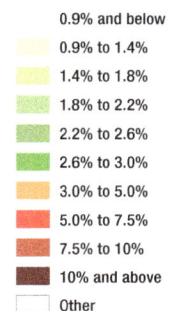

0.9% and below
0.9% to 1.4%
1.4% to 1.8%
1.8% to 2.2%
2.2% to 2.6%
2.6% to 3.0%
3.0% to 5.0%
5.0% to 7.5%
7.5% to 10%
10% and above
Other

If consumers economize on their electricity consumption following the implementation of the CPP, the cost burden will increase but by less than under the static scenario. Based on the historical response in the short-term, average expenditures will increase to $1,587 or 2.92 percent of 2014 median household income – 0.86 percent in parts of Richmond County and 11.68 percent in the low-income parts of Onondaga County.

EXPENDITURES
AS A PERCENTAGE
OF MEDIAN
HOUSEHOLD
INCOME:
SHORT-TERM

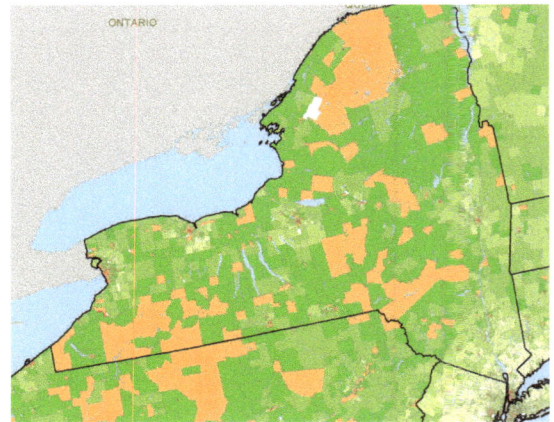

Based on the historical response in the long-term, average expenditures will increase to $1,554 or 2.86 percent of 2014 median household income – 0.84 percent in the upper-income parts of Richmond County and 11.44 percent in the lower-income parts of Onondaga County.

EXPENDITURES AS A PERCENTAGE OF MEDIAN HOUSEHOLD INCOME: LONG-TERM

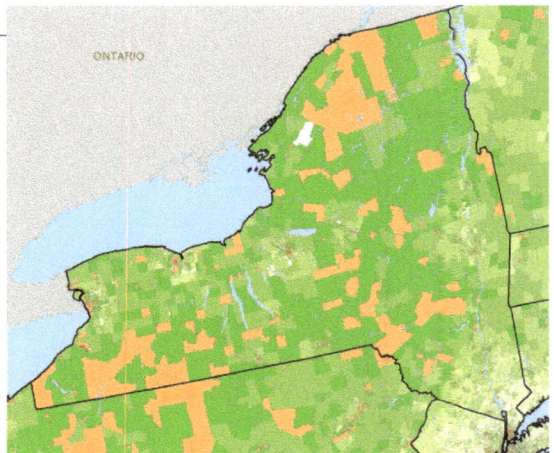

LEGEND

	0.9% and below
	0.9% to 1.4%
	1.4% to 1.8%
	1.8% to 2.2%
	2.2% to 2.6%
	2.6% to 3.0%
	3.0% to 5.0%
	5.0% to 7.5%
	7.5% to 10%
	10% and above
	Other

North Carolina

As of 2014, the average annual expenditures on electricity in North Carolina were $1,513 or 3.23 percent of the 2014 median household income of $46,784. The cost burden ranges from a low of 0.91 percent in parts of Mecklenburg County (median household income of $184,336), to a high of 40.85 percent in low-income parts of Orange County (median household income of $2,500).

2014 EXPENDITURES AS A PERCENTAGE OF MEDIAN HOUSEHOLD INCOME

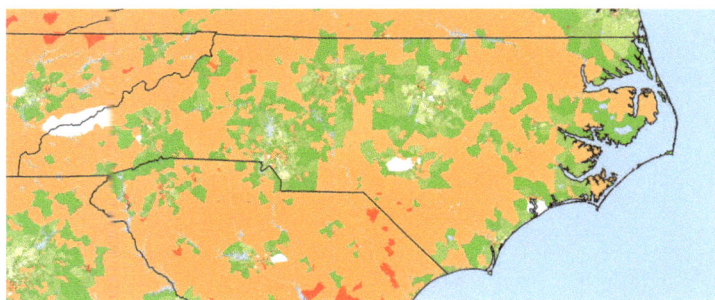

If the CPP is implemented, and consumers do not change their behavior, the cost burden will increase significantly to an average of $1,871 or 4.00 percent of 2014 median household income. In the high-income parts of Mecklenburg County, the burden increases to 1.12 percent, while in the low-income parts of Orange County the burden increases to 50.53 percent.

EXPENDITURES AS A PERCENTAGE OF MEDIAN HOUSEHOLD INCOME: STATIC ANALYSIS

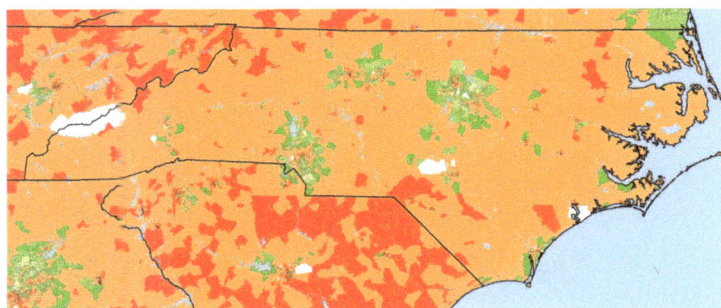

"Not only will these new federal rules raise electricity rates, they have the potential to jeopardize the success we've made in making North Carolina's air the cleanest it's been since we began tracking air quality back in the 1970s."

—Gov. Pat McCrory

FACT

North Carolina's poorest families could see average electricity expenditures rise to more than 50 percent of their annual income under the Obama Clean Power Plan.

LEGEND

- 0.9% and below
- 0.9% to 1.4%
- 1.4% to 1.8%
- 1.8% to 2.2%
- 2.2% to 2.6%
- 2.6% to 3.0%
- 3.0% to 5.0%
- 5.0% to 7.5%
- 7.5% to 10%
- 10% and above
- Other

If consumers economize on their electricity consumption following the implementation of the CPP, the cost burden will increase but by less than under the static scenario. Based on the historical response in the short-term, average expenditures will increase to $1,757 or 3.76 percent of 2014 median household income − 1.06 percent in parts of Mecklenburg County and 47.45 percent in the low-income parts of Orange County.

EXPENDITURES AS A PERCENTAGE OF MEDIAN HOUSEHOLD INCOME: SHORT-TERM

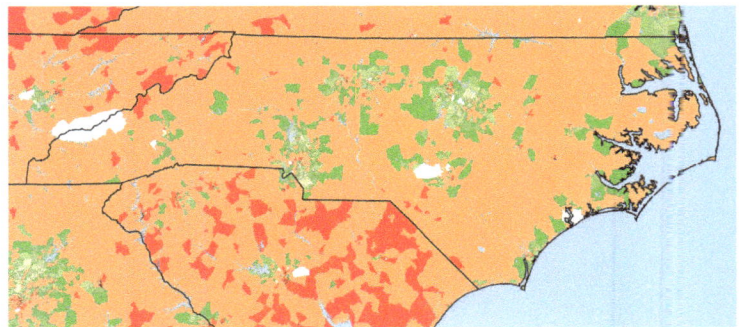

Based on the historical response in the long-term, average expenditures will increase to $1,745 or 3.73 percent of 2014 median household income − 1.05 percent in the upper-income parts of Mecklenburg County and 47.12 percent in the lower-income parts of Orange County.

EXPENDITURES AS A PERCENTAGE OF MEDIAN HOUSEHOLD INCOME: LONG-TERM

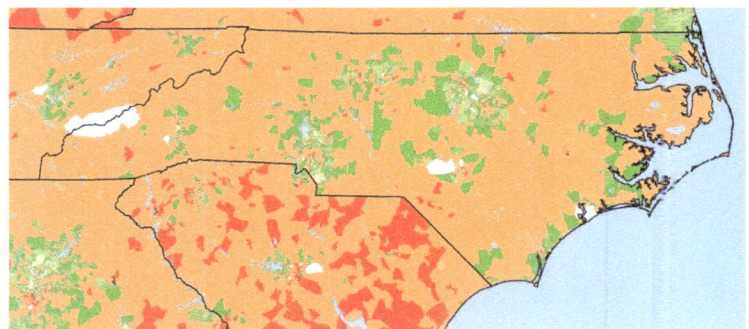

LEGEND

- 0.9% and below
- 0.9% to 1.4%
- 1.4% to 1.8%
- 1.8% to 2.2%
- 2.2% to 2.6%
- 2.6% to 3.0%
- 3.0% to 5.0%
- 5.0% to 7.5%
- 7.5% to 10%
- 10% and above
- Other

North Dakota

As of 2014, the average annual expenditures on electricity in North Dakota were $1,352 or 2.23 percent of the 2014 median household income of $60,730. The cost burden ranges from a low of 1.16 percent in parts of Cass County (median household income of $128,882), to a high of 6.69 percent in low-income parts of Grand Forks County (median household income of $13,656).

2014 EXPENDITURES AS A PERCENTAGE OF MEDIAN HOUSEHOLD INCOME

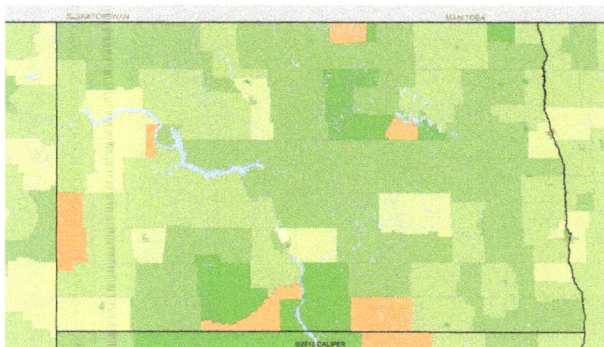

If the CPP is implemented, and consumers do not change their behavior, the cost burden will increase significantly to an average of $1,674 or 2.76 percent of 2014 median household income. In the high-income parts of Cass County, the burden increases to 1.44 percent, while in the low-income parts of Grand Forks County the burden increases to 8.28 percent.

EXPENDITURES AS A PERCENTAGE OF MEDIAN HOUSEHOLD INCOME: STATIC ANALYSIS

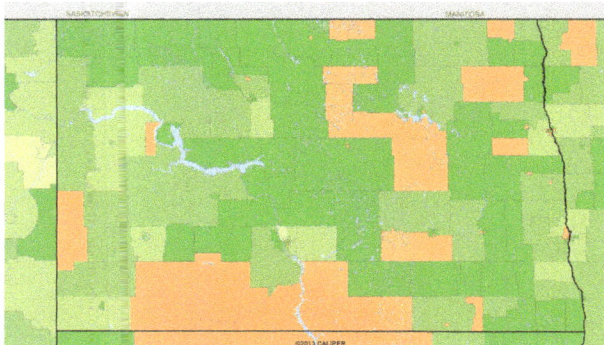

"Approximately 80 percent of North Dakota's electricity is still delivered via coal-fired power and continues to provide some of the most reliable, redundant, and affordable energy to many regions throughout the country. In North Dakota, coal is a critical part of our energy supply - providing some of the lowest electric rates in the country and supporting more than 13,000 jobs in the state."

—Sen. Heidi Heitkamp

FACT

North Dakota residents could soon be paying nearly $1,700 a year on average for electricity under the Obama climate agenda.

LEGEND

- 0.9% and below
- 0.9% to 1.4%
- 1.4% to 1.8%
- 1.8% to 2.2%
- 2.2% to 2.6%
- 2.6% to 3.0%
- 3.0% to 5.0%
- 5.0% to 7.5%
- 7.5% to 10%
- 10% and above
- Other

If consumers economize on their electricity consumption following the implementation of the CPP, the cost burden will increase but by less than under the static scenario. Based on the historical response in the short-term, average expenditures will increase to $1,622 or 2.67 percent of 2014 median household income – 1.39 percent in parts of Cass County and 8.02 percent in the low-income parts of Grand Forks County.

EXPENDITURES AS A PERCENTAGE OF MEDIAN HOUSEHOLD INCOME: SHORT-TERM

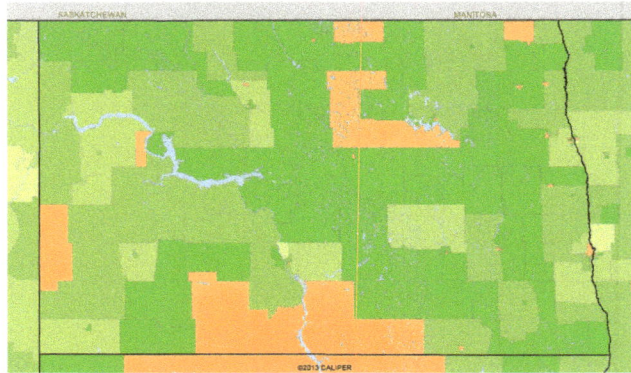

Based on the historical response in the long-term, average expenditures will increase to $1,596 or 2.63 percent of 2014 median household income – 1.37 percent in the upper-income parts of Cass County and 7.89 percent in the lower-income parts of Grand Forks County.

EXPENDITURES AS A PERCENTAGE OF MEDIAN HOUSEHOLD INCOME: LONG-TERM

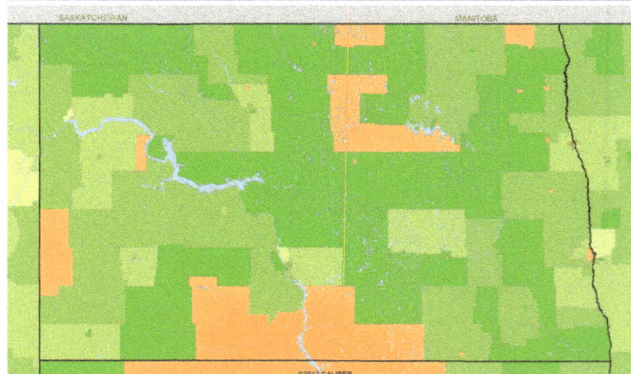

LEGEND

	0.9% and below
	0.9% to 1.4%
	1.4% to 1.8%
	1.8% to 2.2%
	2.2% to 2.6%
	2.6% to 3.0%
	3.0% to 5.0%
	5.0% to 7.5%
	7.5% to 10%
	10% and above
	Other

Ohio

As of 2014, the average annual expenditures on electricity in Ohio were $1,445 or 2.91 percent of the 2014 median household income of $49,644. The cost burden ranges from a low of 0.88 percent in parts of Cuyahoga County (median household income of $181,500), to a high of 27.85 percent in low-income parts of Athens County (median household income of $3,502).

2014 EXPENDITURES AS A PERCENTAGE OF MEDIAN HOUSEHOLD INCOME

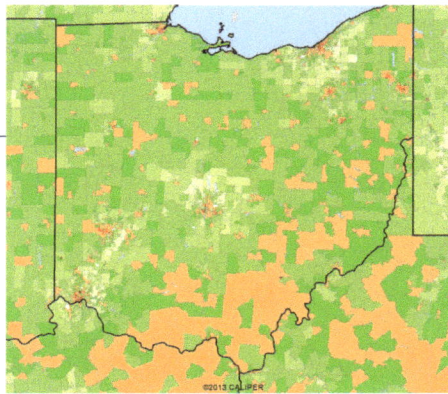

If the CPP is implemented, and consumers do not change their behavior, the cost burden will increase significantly to an average of $1,895 or 3.82 percent of 2014 median household income. In the high-income parts of Cuyahoga County, the burden increases to 1.16 percent, while in the low-income parts of Athens County the burden increases to 36.54 percent.

EXPENDITURES AS A PERCENTAGE OF MEDIAN HOUSEHOLD INCOME: STATIC ANALYSIS

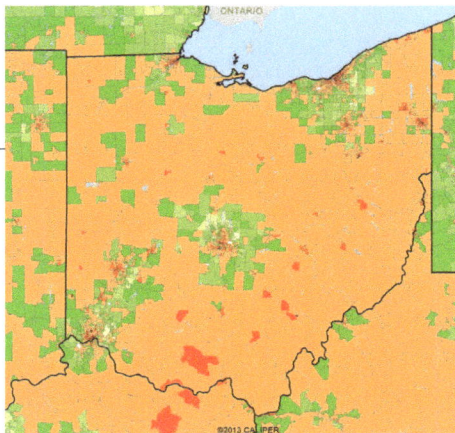

"This regulation . . . has the potential to cost Ohio's electric cooperative members hundreds of dollars a year on their electric bills while providing little, if any, environmental benefit."

—Pat O'Loughlin, President and CEO of Buckeye Power

FACT

Ohio's poorest residents in Athens County could soon see average electricity expenditures skyrocket to 36.54 percent of their annual income under the Obama Clean Power Plan.

LEGEND

- 0.9% and below
- 0.9% to 1.4%
- 1.4% to 1.8%
- 1.8% to 2.2%
- 2.2% to 2.6%
- 2.6% to 3.0%
- 3.0% to 5.0%
- 5.0% to 7.5%
- 7.5% to 10%
- 10% and above
- Other

If consumers economize on their electricity consumption following the implementation of the CPP, the cost burden will increase but by less than under the static scenario. Based on the historical response in the short-term, average expenditures will increase to $1,822 or 3.67 percent of 2014 median household income − 1.11 percent in parts of Cuyahoga County and 35.13 percent in the low-income parts of Athens County.

EXPENDITURES AS A
PERCENTAGE OF MEDIAN
HOUSEHOLD INCOME:
SHORT-TERM

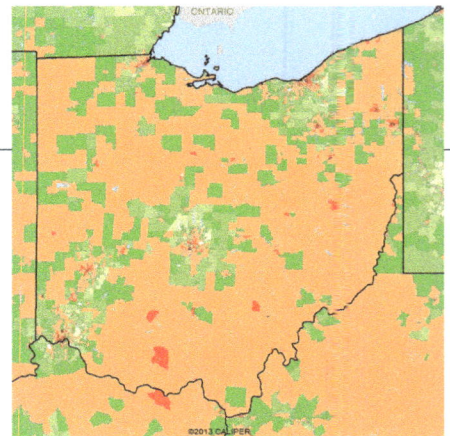

Based on the historical response in the long-term, average expenditures will increase to $1,785 or 3.60 percent of 2014 median household income − 1.09 percent in the upper-income parts of Cuyahoga County and 34.42 percent in the lower-income parts of Athens County.

EXPENDITURES AS A
PERCENTAGE OF MEDIAN
HOUSEHOLD INCOME:
LONG-TERM

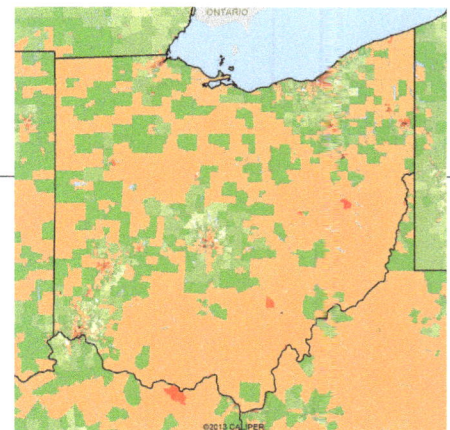

LEGEND

	0.9% and below
	0.9% to 1.4%
	1.4% to 1.8%
	1.8% to 2.2%
	2.2% to 2.6%
	2.6% to 3.0%
	3.0% to 5.0%
	5.0% to 7.5%
	7.5% to 10%
	10% and above
	Other

Oklahoma

As of 2014, the average annual expenditures on electricity in Oklahoma were $1,374 or 2.91 percent of the 2014 median household income of $47,199. The cost burden ranges from a low of 1.00 percent in parts of Tulsa County (median household income of $152,330), to a high of 14.85 percent in low-income parts of Cleveland County (median household income of $6,250).

2014 EXPENDITURES AS A PERCENTAGE OF MEDIAN HOUSEHOLD INCOME

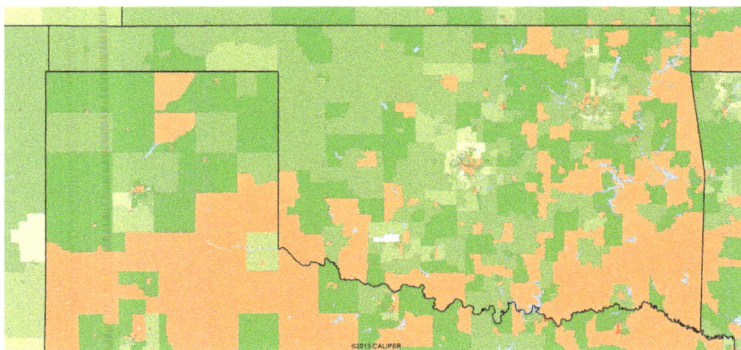

If the CPP is implemented, and consumers do not change their behavior, the cost burden will increase significantly to an average of $1,724 or 3.65 percent of 2014 median household income. In the high-income parts of Tulsa County, the burden increases to 1.25 percent, while in the low-income parts of Cleveland County the burden increases to 18.62 percent.

EXPENDITURES AS A PERCENTAGE OF MEDIAN HOUSEHOLD INCOME: STATIC ANALYSIS

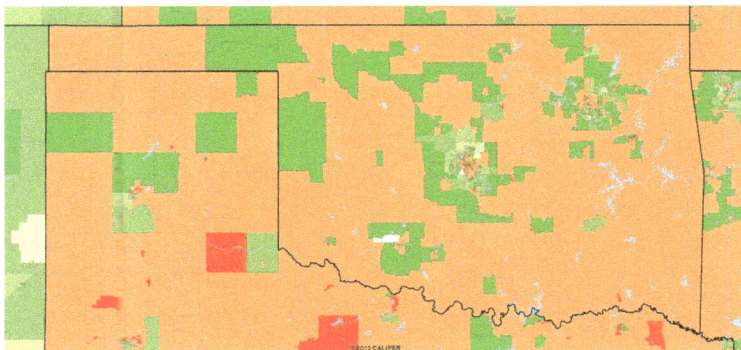

FACTS

- Oklahoma families could see their power bills rise to $1,724 per year on average under the Obama Climate agenda.

- Low-income residents in Cleveland County could see average electricity expenditures increase to 18.62 percent of their annual income.

- Harmon, Latimer, and Nowata County residents could see their annual power bills go up by 20.4 percent.

LEGEND

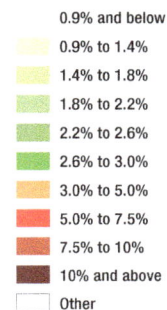

0.9% and below
0.9% to 1.4%
1.4% to 1.8%
1.8% to 2.2%
2.2% to 2.6%
2.6% to 3.0%
3.0% to 5.0%
5.0% to 7.5%
7.5% to 10%
10% and above
Other

If consumers economize on their electricity consumption following the implementation of the CPP, the cost burden will increase but by less than under the static scenario. Based on the historical response in the short-term, average expenditures will increase to $1,679 or 3.56 percent of 2014 median household income – 1.22 percent in parts of Tulsa County and 18.14 percent in the low-income parts of Cleveland County.

EXPENDITURES AS A PERCENTAGE OF MEDIAN HOUSEHOLD INCOME SHORT-TERM

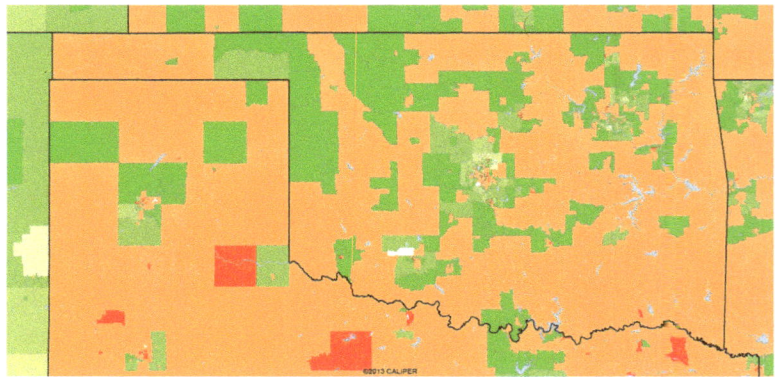

Based on the historical response in the long-term, average expenditures will increase to $1,663 or 3.52 percent of 2014 median household income – 1.21 percent in the upper-income parts of Tulsa County and 17.96 percent in the lower-income parts of Cleveland County.

EXPENDITURES AS A PERCENTAGE OF MEDIAN HOUSEHOLD INCOME: LONG-TERM

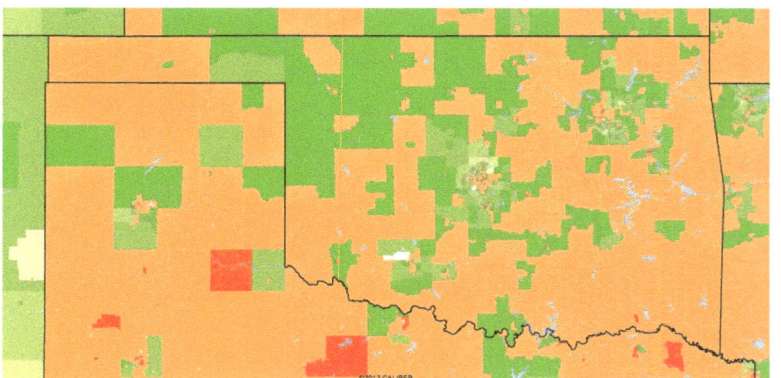

LEGEND

- 0.9% and below
- 0.9% to 1.4%
- 1.4% to 1.8%
- 1.8% to 2.2%
- 2.2% to 2.6%
- 2.6% to 3.0%
- 3.0% to 5.0%
- 5.0% to 7.5%
- 7.5% to 10%
- 10% and above
- Other

Oregon

As of 2014, the average annual expenditures on electricity in Oregon were $1,163 or 1.98 percent of the 2014 median household income of $58,875. The cost burden ranges from a low of 0.77 percent in parts of Multnomah County (median household income of $166,278), to a high of 9.54 percent in low-income parts of Lane County (median household income of $8,235).

2014
EXPENDITURES
AS A PERCENTAGE
OF MEDIAN
HOUSEHOLD
INCOME

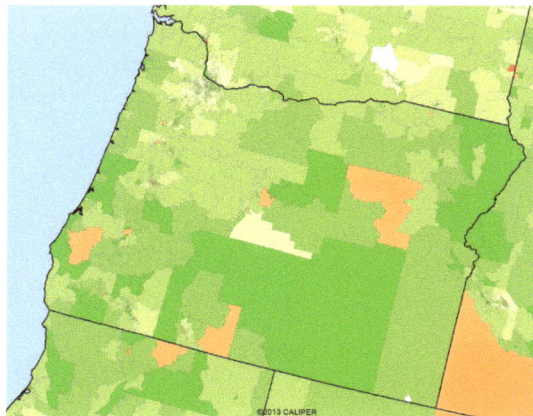

If the CPP is implemented, and consumers do not change their behavior, the cost burden will increase significantly to an average of $1,312 or 2.23 percent of 2014 median household income. In the high-income parts of Multnomah County, the burden increases to 0.87 percent, while in the low-income parts of Lane County the burden increases to 10.76 percent.

EXPENDITURES
AS A PERCENTAGE
OF MEDIAN
HOUSEHOLD
INCOME: STATIC
ANALYSIS

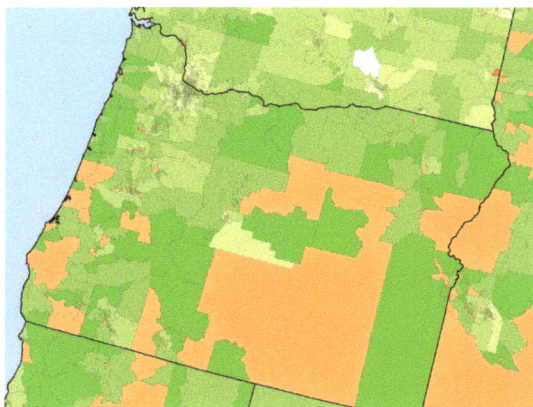

LEGEND

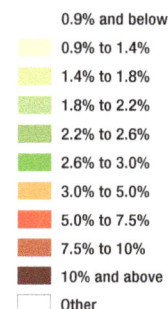

0.9% and below
0.9% to 1.4%
1.4% to 1.8%
1.8% to 2.2%
2.2% to 2.6%
2.6% to 3.0%
3.0% to 5.0%
5.0% to 7.5%
7.5% to 10%
10% and above
Other

If consumers economize on their electricity consumption following the implementation of the CPP, the cost burden will increase but by less than under the static scenario. Based on the historical response in the short-term, average expenditures will increase to $1,284 or 2.18 percent of 2014 median household income – 0.86 percent in parts of Multnomah County and 10.53 percent in the low-income parts of Lane County.

EXPENDITURES AS
A PERCENTAGE OF
MEDIAN HOUSEHOLD
INCOME: SHORT-TERM

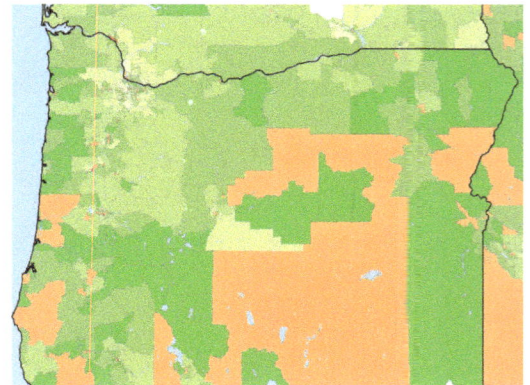

Based on the historical response in the long-term, average expenditures will increase to $1,274 or 2.16 percent of 2014 median household income – 0.85 percent in the upper-income parts of Multnomah County and 10.45 percent in the lower-income parts of Lane County.

LEGEND

- 0.9% and below
- 0.9% to 1.4%
- 1.4% to 1.8%
- 1.8% to 2.2%
- 2.2% to 2.6%
- 2.6% to 3.0%
- 3.0% to 5.0%
- 5.0% to 7.5%
- 7.5% to 10%
- 10% and above
- Other

EXPENDITURES AS
A PERCENTAGE OF
MEDIAN HOUSEHOLD
INCOME: LONG-TERM

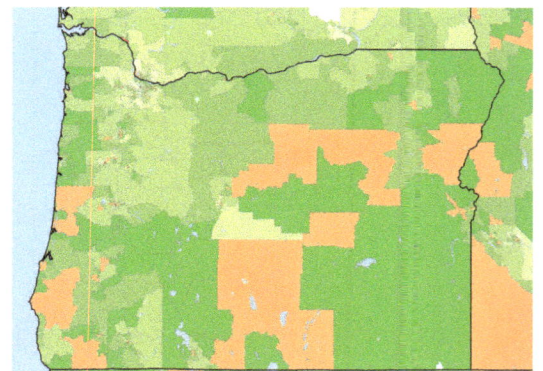

Pennsylvania

As of 2014, the average annual expenditures on electricity in Pennsylvania were $1,241 or 2.25 percent of the 2014 median household income of $55,173. The cost burden ranges from a low of 0.74 percent in parts of Montgomery County (median household income of $204,297), to a high of 17.44 percent in low-income parts of Indiana County (median household income of $4,801).

2014 EXPENDITURES AS A PERCENTAGE OF MEDIAN HOUSEHOLD INCOME

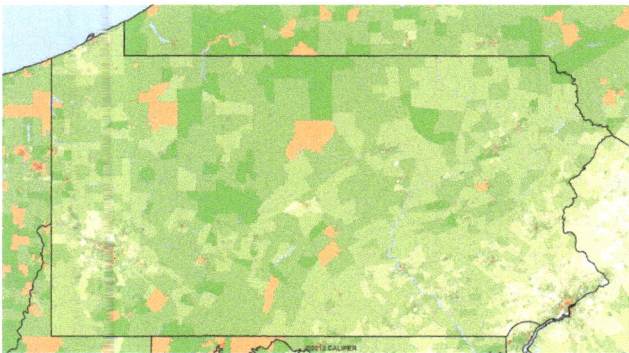

If the CPP is implemented, and consumers do not change their behavior, the cost burden will increase significantly to an average of $1,567 or 2.84 percent of 2014 median household income. In the high-income parts of Multnomah County, the burden increases to 0.94 percent, while in the low-income parts of Lane County the burden increases to 22.03 percent.

EXPENDITURES AS A PERCENTAGE OF MEDIAN HOUSEHOLD INCOME: STATIC ANALYSIS

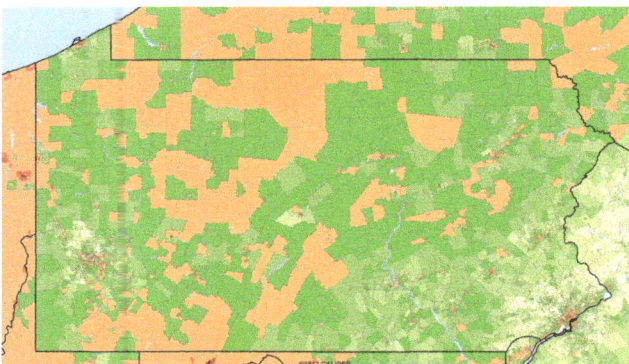

"Make no mistake; there is a war on coal. It's also a war on consumers, affordable electricity, and American jobs."

—Congressman Glenn Thompson (R-PA)

FACT

Pennsylvania families could soon be spending $1,567 a year on average for electricity under the proposed Clean Power Plan.

LEGEND

- 0.9% and below
- 0.9% to 1.4%
- 1.4% to 1.8%
- 1.8% to 2.2%
- 2.2% to 2.6%
- 2.6% to 3.0%
- 3.0% to 5.0%
- 5.0% to 7.5%
- 7.5% to 10%
- 10% and above
- Other

If consumers economize on their electricity consumption following the implementation of the CPP, the cost burden will increase but by less than under the static scenario. Based on the historical response in the short-term, average expenditures will increase to $1,504 or 2.73 percent of 2014 median household income – 0.90 percent in parts of Multnomah County and 21.15 percent in the low-income parts of Lane County.

EXPENDITURES AS A PERCENTAGE OF MEDIAN HOUSEHOLD INCOME: SHORT-TERM

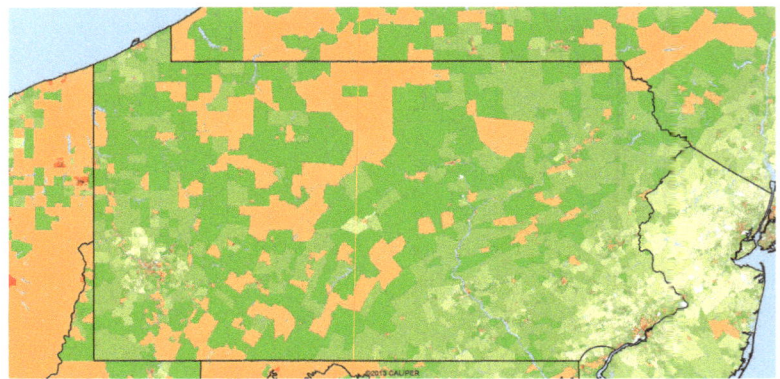

Based on the historical response in the long-term, average expenditures will increase to $1,461 or 2.65 percent of 2014 median household income – 0.88 percent in the upper-income parts of Multnomah County and 20.54 percent in the lower-income parts of Lane County.

EXPENDITURES AS A PERCENTAGE OF MEDIAN HOUSEHOLD INCOME: LONG-TERM

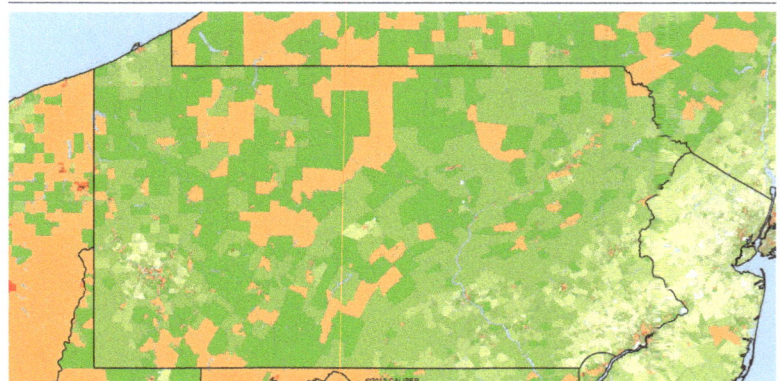

LEGEND

	0.9% and below
	0.9% to 1.4%
	1.4% to 1.8%
	1.8% to 2.2%
	2.2% to 2.6%
	2.6% to 3.0%
	3.0% to 5.0%
	5.0% to 7.5%
	7.5% to 10%
	10% and above
	Other

Rhode Island

As of 2014, the average annual expenditures on electricity in Rhode Island were $1,186 or 2.02 percent of the 2014 median household income of $58,633. The cost burden ranges from a low of 0.93 percent in parts of Bristol County (median household income of $141,467), to a high of 6.96 percent in low-income parts of Providence County (median household income of $11,498).

2014 EXPENDITURES AS A PERCENTAGE OF MEDIAN HOUSEHOLD INCOME

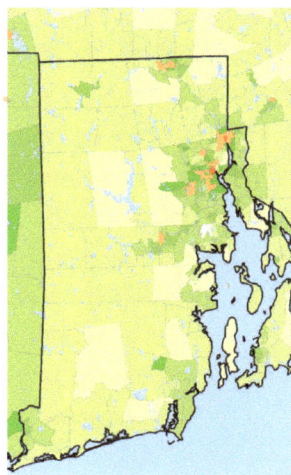

If the CPP is implemented, and consumers do not change their behavior, the cost burden will increase significantly to an average of $1,380 or 2.35 percent of 2014 median household income. In the high-income parts of Bristol County, the burden increases to 1.08 percent, while in the low-income parts of Providence County the burden increases to 8.10 percent.

EXPENDITURES AS A PERCENTAGE OF MEDIAN HOUSEHOLD INCOME: STATIC ANALYSIS

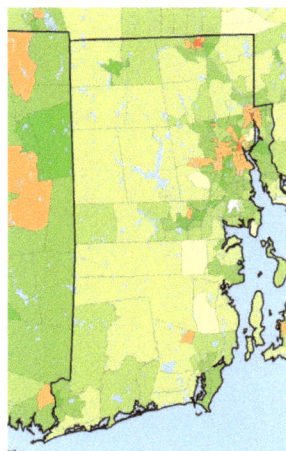

LEGEND

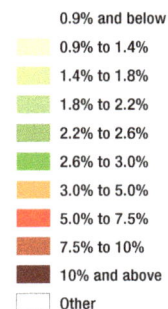

- 0.9% and below
- 0.9% to 1.4%
- 1.4% to 1.8%
- 1.8% to 2.2%
- 2.2% to 2.6%
- 2.6% to 3.0%
- 3.0% to 5.0%
- 5.0% to 7.5%
- 7.5% to 10%
- 10% and above
- Other

If consumers economize on their electricity consumption following the implementation of the CPP, the cost burden will increase but by less than under the static scenario. Based on the historical response in the short-term, average expenditures will increase to $1,343 or 2.29 percent of 2014 median household income – 1.05 percent in parts of Bristol County and 7.88 percent in the low-income parts of Providence County.

EXPENDITURES AS A PERCENTAGE OF MEDIAN HOUSEHOLD INCOME: SHORT-TERM

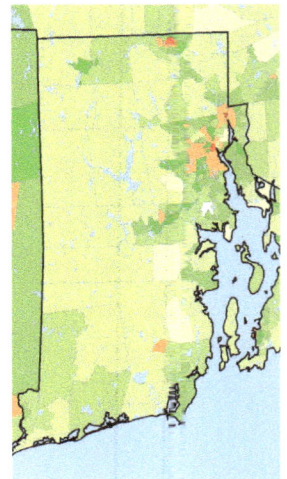

Based on the historical response in the long-term, average expenditures will increase to $1,317 or 2.25 percent of 2014 median household income – 1.03 percent in the upper-income parts of Bristol County and 7.73 percent in the lower-income parts of Providence County.

EXPENDITURES AS A PERCENTAGE OF MEDIAN HOUSEHOLD INCOME: LONG-TERM

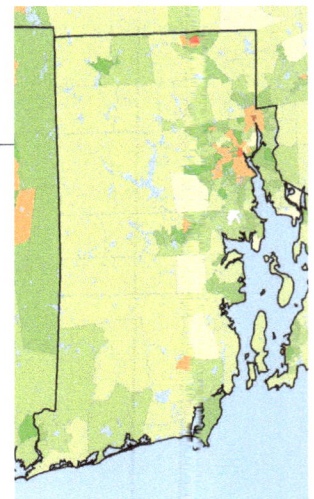

LEGEND

- 0.9% and below
- 0.9% to 1.4%
- 1.4% to 1.8%
- 1.8% to 2.2%
- 2.2% to 2.6%
- 2.6% to 3.0%
- 3.0% to 5.0%
- 5.0% to 7.5%
- 7.5% to 10%
- 10% and above
- Other

South Carolina

As of 2014, the average annual expenditures on electricity in South Carolina were $1,774 or 3.95 percent of the 2014 median household income of $44,929. The cost burden ranges from a low of 1.43 percent in parts of Greenville County (median household income of $137,768), to a high of 26.14 percent in low-income parts of Pickens County (median household income of $4,583).

2014 EXPENDITURES AS A PERCENTAGE OF MEDIAN HOUSEHOLD INCOME

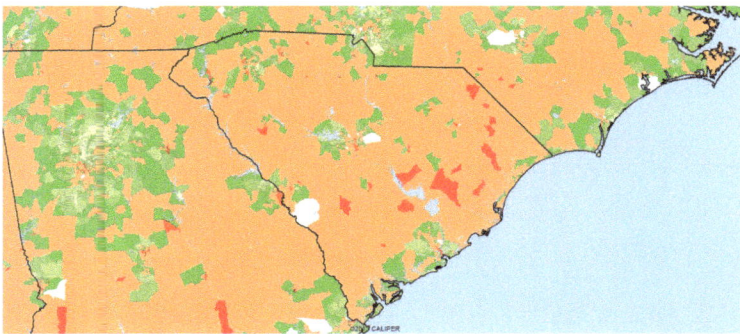

If the CPP is implemented, and consumers do not change their behavior, the cost burden will increase significantly to an average of $2,195 or 4.89 percent of 2014 median household income. In the high-income parts of Greenville County, the burden increases to 1.76 percent, while in the low-income parts of Pickens County the burden increases to 32.33 percent.

EXPENDITURES AS A PERCENTAGE OF MEDIAN HOUSEHOLD INCOME:
STATIC ANALYSIS

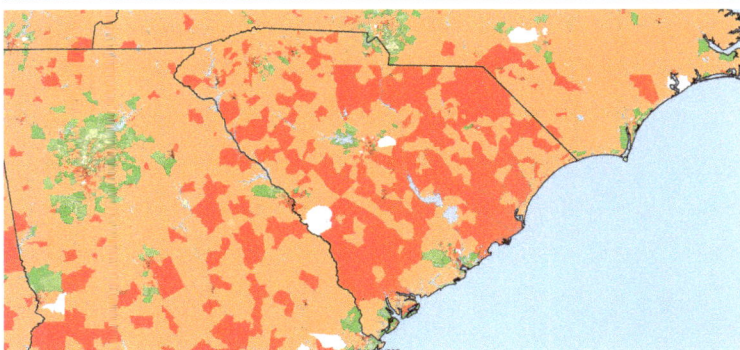

LEGEND

- 0.9% and below
- 0.9% to 1.4%
- 1.4% to 1.8%
- 1.8% to 2.2%
- 2.2% to 2.6%
- 2.6% to 3.0%
- 3.0% to 5.0%
- 5.0% to 7.5%
- 7.5% to 10%
- 10% and above
- Other

If consumers economize on their electricity consumption following the implementation of the CPP, the cost burden will increase but by less than under the static scenario. Based on the historical response in the short-term, average expenditures will increase to $2,061 or 4.59 percent of 2014 median household income – 1.66 percent in parts of Greenville County and 30.36 percent in the low-income parts of Pickens County.

EXPENDITURES AS A PERCENTAGE OF MEDIAN HOUSEHOLD INCOME SHORT-TERM

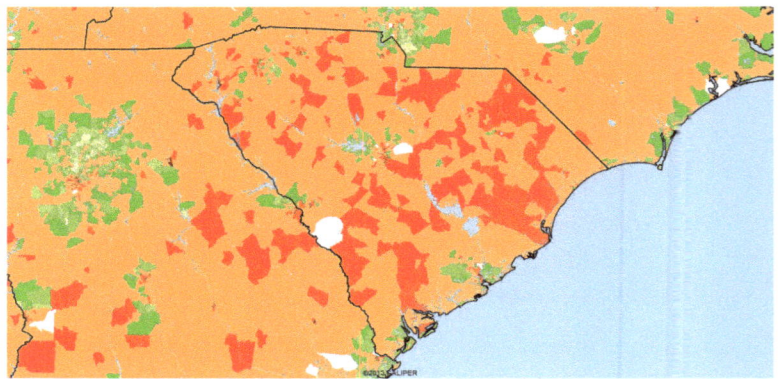

Based on the historical response in the long-term, average expenditures will increase to $2,047 or 4.56 percent of 2014 median household income – 1.65 percent in the upper-income parts of Greenville County and 30.15 percent in the lower-income parts of Pickens County.

EXPENDITURES AS A PERCENTAGE OF MEDIAN HOUSEHOLD INCOME LONG-TERM

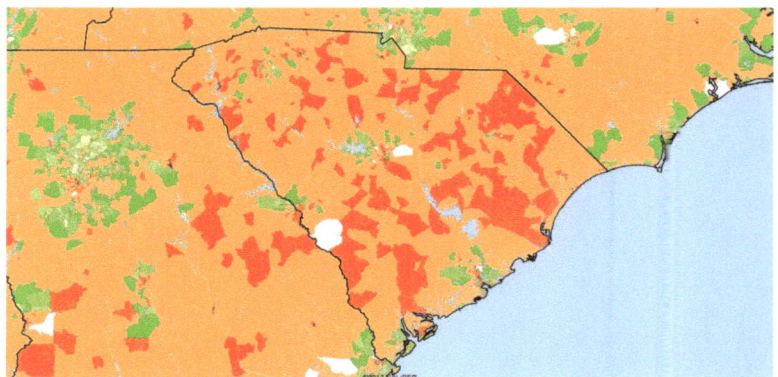

LEGEND

	0.9% and below
	0.9% to 1.4%
	1.4% to 1.8%
	1.8% to 2.2%
	2.2% to 2.6%
	2.6% to 3.0%
	3.0% to 5.0%
	5.0% to 7.5%
	7.5% to 10%
	10% and above
	Other

South Dakota

As of 2014, the average annual expenditures on electricity in South Dakota were $1,311 or 2.47 percent of the 2014 median household income of $53,053. The cost burden ranges from a low of 1.29 percent in parts of Lincoln County (median household income of $112,750), to a high of 4.26 percent in low-income parts of Pennington County (median household income of $20,778).

2014 EXPENDITURES AS A PERCENTAGE OF MEDIAN HOUSEHOLD INCOME

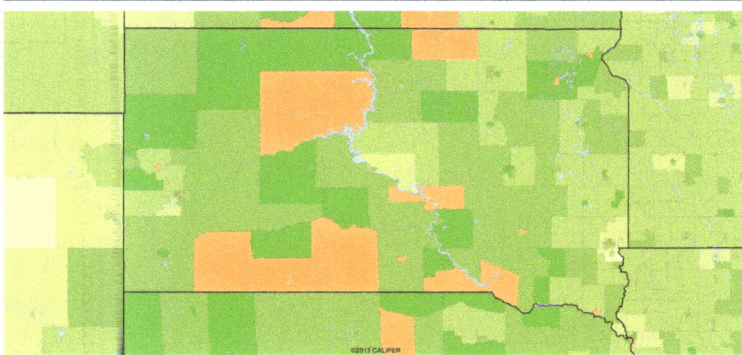

If the CPP is implemented, and consumers do not change their behavior, the cost burden will increase significantly to an average of $1,623 or 3.06 percent of 2014 median household income. In the high-income parts of Lincoln County, the burden increases to 1.59 percent, while in the low-income parts of Pennington County the burden increases to 5.27 percent.

EXPENDITURES AS A PERCENTAGE OF MEDIAN HOUSEHOLD INCOME: STATIC ANALYSIS

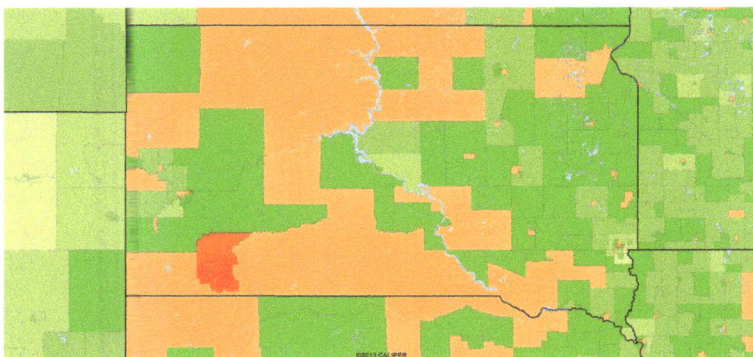

"This rule will have a dramatic impact on the electric bills paid by every South Dakotan. We've worked extremely hard to control costs and keep electricity affordable, but the EPA's plan will simply increase the cost of electricity for every consumer."

—Ed Anderson, Executive Director of South Dakota Rural Electric Association

FACT

South Dakota families could soon be paying $1,623 a year on average for electricity under the Obama climate agenda.

LEGEND

- 0.9% and below
- 0.9% to 1.4%
- 1.4% to 1.8%
- 1.8% to 2.2%
- 2.2% to 2.6%
- 2.6% to 3.0%
- 3.0% to 5.0%
- 5.0% to 7.5%
- 7.5% to 10%
- 10% and above
- Other

If consumers economize on their electricity consumption following the implementation of the CPP, the cost burden will increase but by less than under the static scenario. Based on the historical response in the short-term, average expenditures will increase to $1,572 or 2.96 percent of 2014 median household income – 1.54 percent in parts of Lincoln County and 5.11 percent in the low-income parts of Pennington County.

EXPENDITURES AS A PERCENTAGE OF MEDIAN HOUSEHOLD INCOME: SHORT-TERM

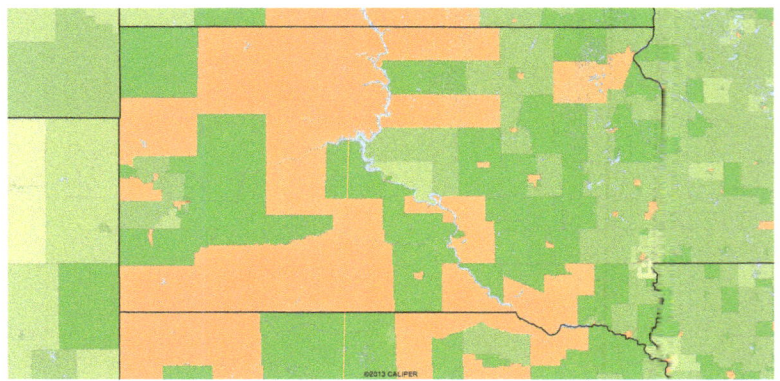

Based on the historical response in the long-term, average expenditures will increase to $1,547 or 2.92 percent of 2014 median household income – 1.52 percent in the upper-income parts of Lincoln County and 5.03 percent in the lower-income parts of Pennington County.

EXPENDITURES AS A PERCENTAGE OF MEDIAN HOUSEHOLD INCOME: LONG-TERM

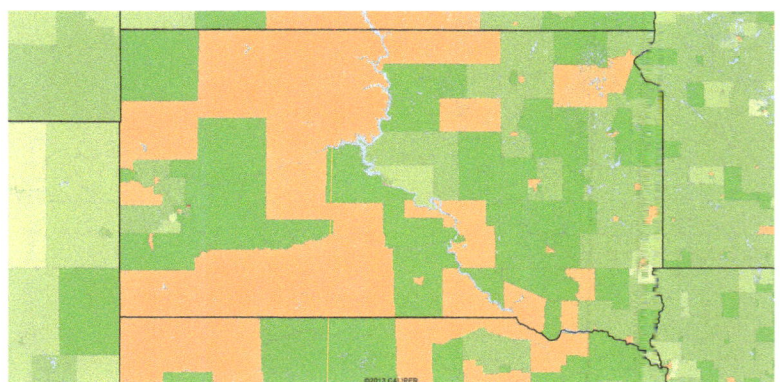

LEGEND

	0.9% and below
	0.9% to 1.4%
	1.4% to 1.8%
	1.8% to 2.2%
	2.2% to 2.6%
	2.6% to 3.0%
	3.0% to 5.0%
	5.0% to 7.5%
	7.5% to 10%
	10% and above
	Other

Tennessee

As of 2014, the average annual expenditures on electricity in Tennessee were $1,593 or 3.64 percent of the 2014 median household income of $43,716. The cost burden ranges from a low of 0.94 percent in parts of Davidson County (median household income of $188,594), to a high of 22.73 percent in low-income parts of Rutherford County (median household income of $4,732).

2014 EXPENDITURES AS A PERCENTAGE OF MEDIAN HOUSEHOLD INCOME

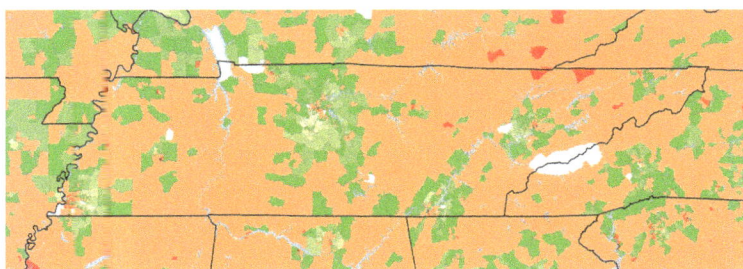

If the CPP is implemented, and consumers do not change their behavior, the cost burden will increase significantly to an average of $2,028 or 4.64 percent of 2014 median household income. In the high-income parts of Davidson County, the burden increases to 1.19 percent, while in the low-income parts of Rutherford County the burden increases to 28.93 percent.

EXPENDITURES AS A PERCENTAGE OF MEDIAN HOUSEHOLD INCOME: STATIC ANALYSIS

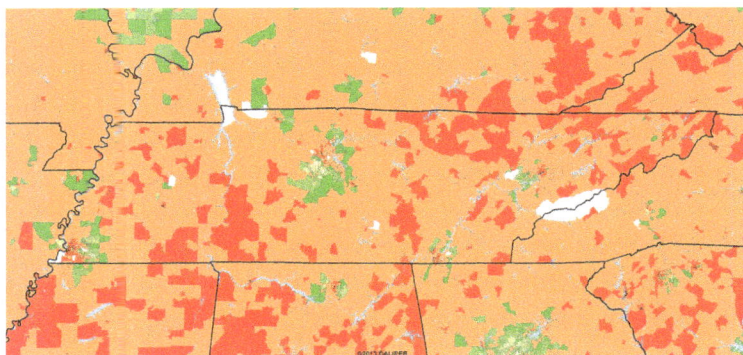

LEGEND

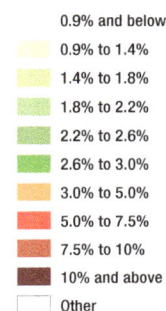

	0.9% and below
	0.9% to 1.4%
	1.4% to 1.8%
	1.8% to 2.2%
	2.2% to 2.6%
	2.6% to 3.0%
	3.0% to 5.0%
	5.0% to 7.5%
	7.5% to 10%
	10% and above
	Other

If consumers economize on their electricity consumption following the implementation of the CPP, the cost burden will increase but by less than under the static scenario. Based on the historical response in the short-term, average expenditures will increase to $1,912 or 4.37 percent of 2014 median household income – 1.12 percent in parts of Davidson County and 27.28 percent in the low-income parts of Rutherford County

EXPENDITURES AS A PERCENTAGE OF MEDIAN HOUSEHOLD INCOME:
SHORT-TERM

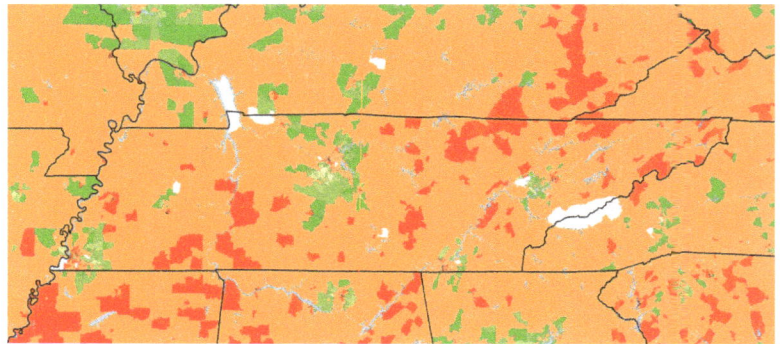

Based on the historical response in the long-term, average expenditures will increase to $1,759 or 4.02 percent of 2014 median household income – 1.03 percent in the upper-income parts of Davidson County and 25.10 percent in the lower-income parts of Rutherford County.

EXPENDITURES AS A PERCENTAGE OF MEDIAN HOUSEHOLD INCOME:
LONG-TERM

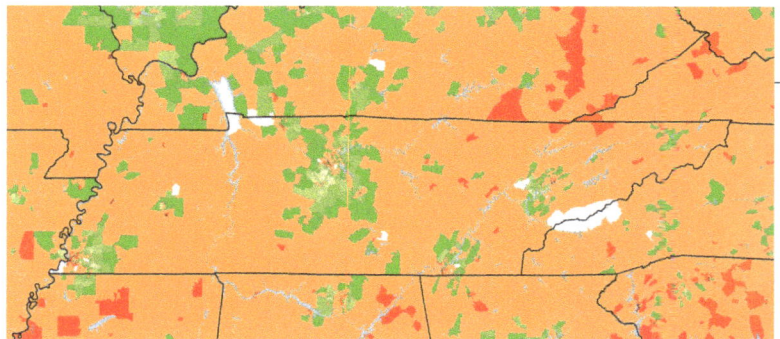

LEGEND

- 0.9% and below
- 0.9% to 1.4%
- 1.4% to 1.8%
- 1.8% to 2.2%
- 2.2% to 2.6%
- 2.6% to 3.0%
- 3.0% to 5.0%
- 5.0% to 7.5%
- 7.5% to 10%
- 10% and above
- Other

Texas

As of 2014, the average annual expenditures on electricity in Texas were $1,650 or 3.06 percent of the 2014 median household income of $53,875. The cost burden ranges from a low of 0.90 percent in parts of Dallas County (median household income of at least $250,000), to a high of 21.44 percent in low-income parts of McLennan County (median household income of $5,196).

2014 EXPENDITURES AS A
PERCENTAGE OF MEDIAN
HOUSEHOLD INCOME

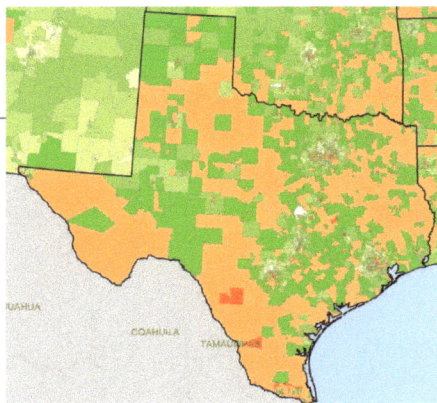

If the CPP is implemented, and consumers do not change their behavior, the cost burden will increase significantly to an average of $1,965 or 3.65 percent of 2014 median household income. In the high-income parts of Dallas County, the burden increases to 1.07 percent, while in the low-income parts of McLennan County the burden increases to 25.53 percent.

EXPENDITURES AS A PERCENTAGE OF MEDIAN HOUSEHOLD INCOME:
STATIC ANALYSIS

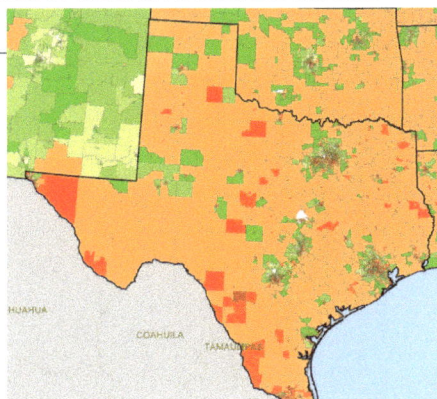

"Recently, the EPA negatively impacted business activity in my district and across the country by implementing a Clean Power Plan and new ozone standards that do not take into account the costs or economic impacts of implementation."

—Congressman
Henry Cuellar (D-TX)

FACT

Texas families could soon be paying nearly $2,000 a year for power on average under the Obama climate agenda.

LEGEND

	0.9% and below
	0.9% to 1.4%
	1.4% to 1.8%
	1.8% to 2.2%
	2.2% to 2.6%
	2.6% to 3.0%
	3.0% to 5.0%
	5.0% to 7.5%
	7.5% to 10%
	10% and above
	Other

If consumers economize on their electricity consumption following the implementation of the CPP, the cost burden will increase but by less than under the static scenario. Based on the historical response in the short-term, average expenditures will increase to $1,925 or 3.57 percent of 2014 median household income − 1.04 percent in parts of Dallas County and 25.01 percent in the low-income parts of McLennan County.

EXPENDITURES AS A PERCENTAGE
OF MEDIAN HOUSEHOLD INCOME:
SHORT-TERM

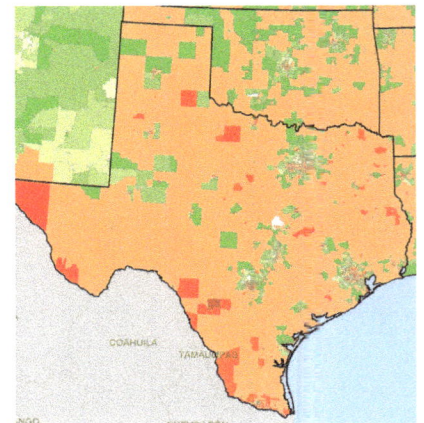

Based on the historical response in the long-term, average expenditures will increase to $1,910 or 3.55 percent of 2014 median household income − 1.04 percent in the upper-income parts of Dallas County and 24.82 percent in the lower-income parts of McLennan County.

EXPENDITURES AS A PERCENTAGE
OF MEDIAN HOUSEHOLD INCOME:
LONG-TERM

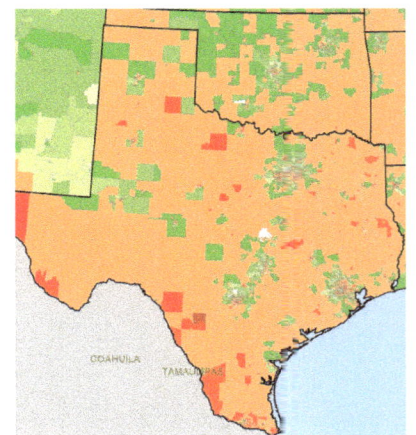

LEGEND

	0.9% and below
	0.9% to 1.4%
	1.4% to 1.8%
	1.8% to 2.2%
	2.2% to 2.6%
	2.6% to 3.0%
	3.0% to 5.0%
	5.0% to 7.5%
	7.5% to 10%
	10% and above
	Other

Utah

As of 2014, the average annual expenditures on electricity in Utah were $962 or 1.52 percent of the 2014 median household income of $63,383. The cost burden ranges from a low of 0.66 percent in parts of Salt Lake County (median household income of $197,000), to a high of 4.30 percent in low-income parts of Utah County (median household income of $15,102).

- Utah families could soon be paying $1,077 yearly on average for electricity under the Obama Clean Power Plan.

- Residents of poor communities in Utah County could soon see their average annual electricity expenditures jump to nearly 5 percent of their annual income.

- Salt Lake County and Sanpete County residents could see their annual electricity costs rise by 10.8 percent.

2014 EXPENDITURES AS A PERCENTAGE OF MEDIAN HOUSEHOLD INCOME

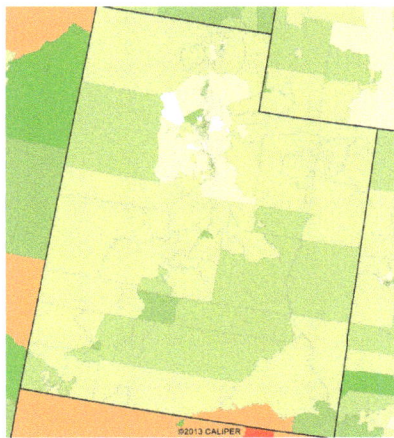

If the CPP is implemented, and consumers do not change their behavior, the cost burden will increase significantly to an average of $1,077 or 1.70 percent of 2014 median household income. In the high-income parts of Salt Lake County, the burden increases to 0.74 percent, while in the low-income parts of Utah County the burden increases to 4.81 percent.

EXPENDITURES AS A PERCENTAGE OF MEDIAN HOUSEHOLD INCOME: STATIC ANALYSIS

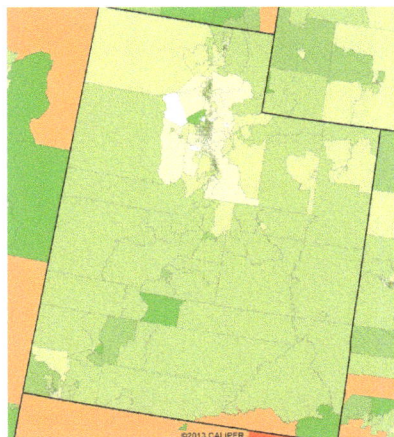

LEGEND

0.9% and below
0.9% to 1.4%
1.4% to 1.8%
1.8% to 2.2%
2.2% to 2.6%
2.6% to 3.0%
3.0% to 5.0%
5.0% to 7.5%
7.5% to 10%
10% and above
Other

If consumers economize on their electricity consumption following the implementation of the CPP, the cost burden will increase but by less than under the static scenario. Based on the historical response in the short-term, average expenditures will increase to $1,053 or 1.66 percent of 2014 median household income − 0.72 percent in parts of Salt Lake County and 4.71 percent in the low-income parts of Utah County.

EXPENDITURES AS A
PERCENTAGE OF MEDIAN
HOUSEHOLD INCOME:
SHORT-TERM

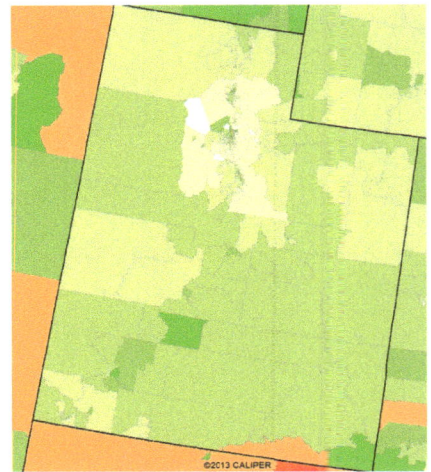

Based on the historical response in the long-term, average expenditures will increase to $1,046 or 1.65 percent of 2014 median household income − 0.72 percent in the upper-income parts of Salt Lake County and 4.68 percent in the lower-income parts of Utah County.

EXPENDITURES AS A
PERCENTAGE OF MEDIAN
HOUSEHOLD INCOME:
LONG-TERM

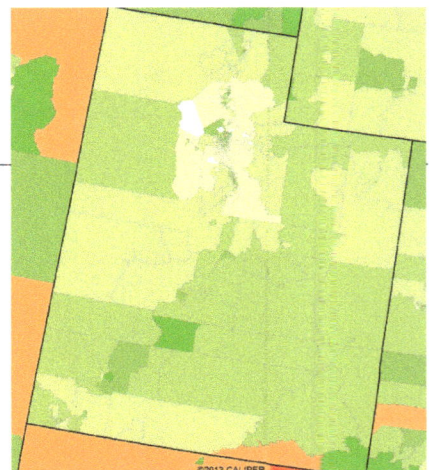

LEGEND

	0.9% and below
	0.9% to 1.4%
	1.4% to 1.8%
	1.8% to 2.2%
	2.2% to 2.6%
	2.6% to 3.0%
	3.0% to 5.0%
	5.0% to 7.5%
	7.5% to 10%
	10% and above
	Other

Vermont

As of 2014, the average annual expenditures on electricity in Vermont were $1,189 or 1.96 percent of the 2014 median household income of $60,708. The cost burden ranges from a low of 1.05 percent in parts of Chittenden County (median household income of $125,294), to a high of 3.44 percent in low-income parts of Windsor County (median household income of $23,333).

2014 EXPENDITURES AS A PERCENTAGE OF MEDIAN HOUSEHOLD INCOME

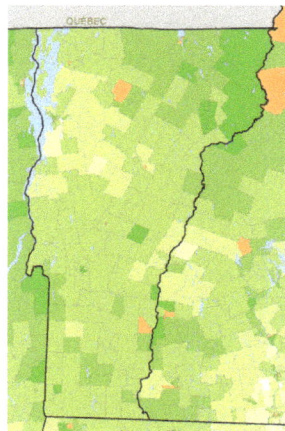

If the CPP is implemented, and consumers do not change their behavior, the cost burden will increase significantly to an average of $1,370 or 2.26 percent of 2014 median household income. In the high-income parts of Chittenden County, the burden increases to 1.21percent, while in the low-income parts of Windsor County the burden increases to 3.97 percent.

EXPENDITURES AS A PERCENTAGE OF MEDIAN HOUSEHOLD INCOME: STATIC ANALYSIS

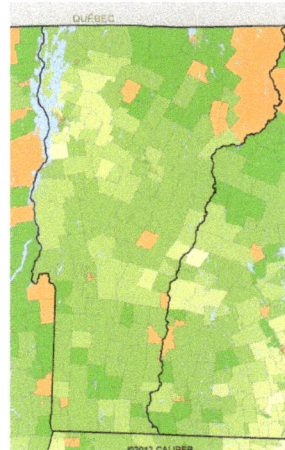

LEGEND

- 0.9% and below
- 0.9% to 1.4%
- 1.4% to 1.8%
- 1.8% to 2.2%
- 2.2% to 2.6%
- 2.6% to 3.0%
- 3.0% to 5.0%
- 5.0% to 7.5%
- 7.5% to 10%
- 10% and above
- Other

If consumers economize on their electricity consumption following the implementation of the CPP, the cost burden will increase but by less than under the static scenario. Based on the historical response in the short-term, average expenditures will increase to $1,335 or 2.20 percent of 2014 median household income – 1.18 percent in parts of Chittenden County and 3.86 percent in the low-income parts of Windsor County.

EXPENDITURES AS A PERCENTAGE OF
MEDIAN HOUSEHOLD INCOME:
SHORT-TERM

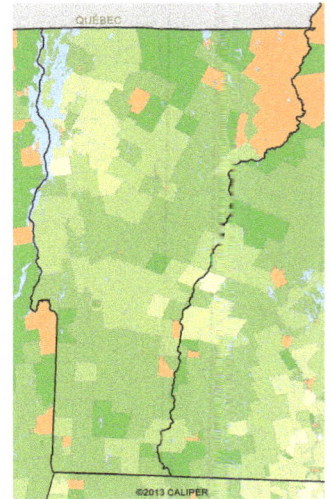

Based on the historical response in the long-term, average expenditures will increase to $1,311 or 2.16 percent of 2014 median household income – 1.15 percent in the upper-income parts of Chittenden County and 3.79 percent in the lower-income parts of Windsor County.

EXPENDITURES AS A PERCENTAGE OF MEDIAN HOUSEHOLD INCOME: LONG-TERM

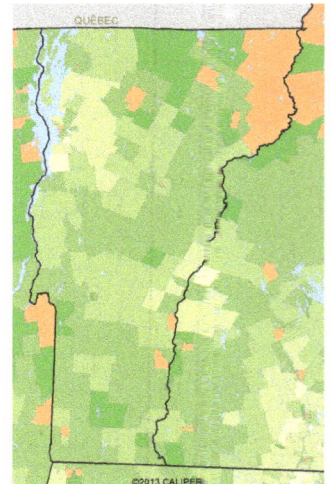

LEGEND

- 0.9% and below
- 0.9% to 1.4%
- 1.4% to 1.8%
- 1.8% to 2.2%
- 2.2% to 2.6%
- 2.6% to 3.0%
- 3.0% to 5.0%
- 5.0% to 7.5%
- 7.5% to 10%
- 10% and above
- Other

Virginia

As of 2014, the average annual expenditures on electricity in Virginia were $1,561 or 2.36 percent of the 2014 median household income of $66,155. The cost burden ranges from a low of 0.85 percent in parts of Fairfax County (median household income of at least $250,000), to a high of 42.14 percent in low-income parts of Albemarle County (median household income of $2,500).

2014 EXPENDITURES AS A PERCENTAGE OF MEDIAN HOUSEHOLD INCOME

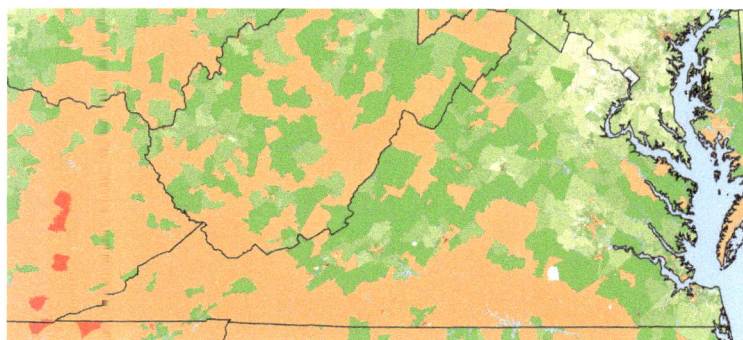

If the CPP is implemented, and consumers do not change their behavior, the cost burden will increase significantly to an average of $1,998 or 3.02 percent of 2014 median household income. In the high-income parts of Fairfax County, the burden increases to 1.08 percent, while in the low-income parts of Albemarle County the burden increases to 53.94 percent.

EXPENDITURES AS A PERCENTAGE OF MEDIAN HOUSEHOLD INCOME: STATIC ANALYSIS

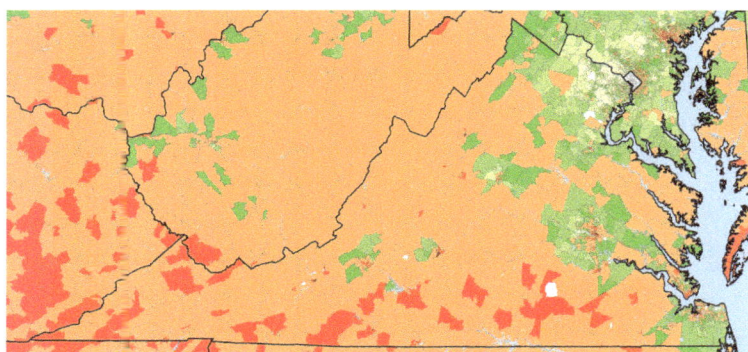

LEGEND

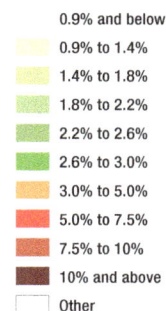

0.9% and below
0.9% to 1.4%
1.4% to 1.8%
1.8% to 2.2%
2.2% to 2.6%
2.6% to 3.0%
3.0% to 5.0%
5.0% to 7.5%
7.5% to 10%
10% and above
Other

If consumers economize on their electricity consumption following the implementation of the CPP, the cost burden will increase but by less than under the static scenario. Based on the historical response in the short-term, average expenditures will increase to $1,859 or 2.81 percent of 2014 median household income – 1.01 percent in parts of Fairfax County and 50.19 percent in the low-income parts of Albemarle County.

EXPENDITURES AS A PERCENTAGE OF MEDIAN HOUSEHOLD INCOME: SHORT-TERM

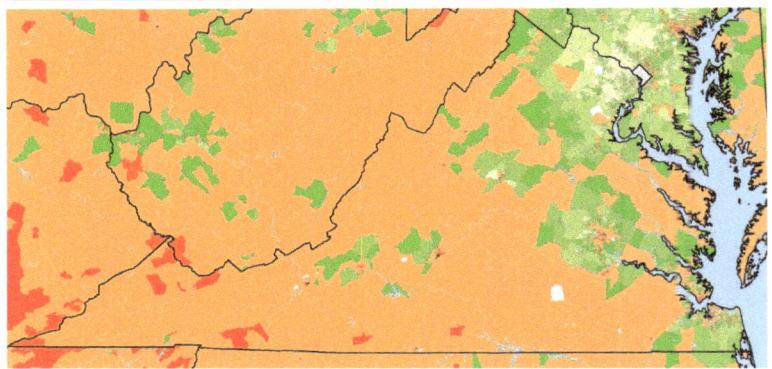

Based on the historical response in the long-term, average expenditures will increase to $1,844 or 2.79 percent of 2014 median household income – 1.00 percent in the upper-income parts of Fairfax County and 49.79 percent in the lower-income parts of Albemarle County.

EXPENDITURES AS A PERCENTAGE OF MEDIAN HOUSEHOLD INCOME: LONG-TERM

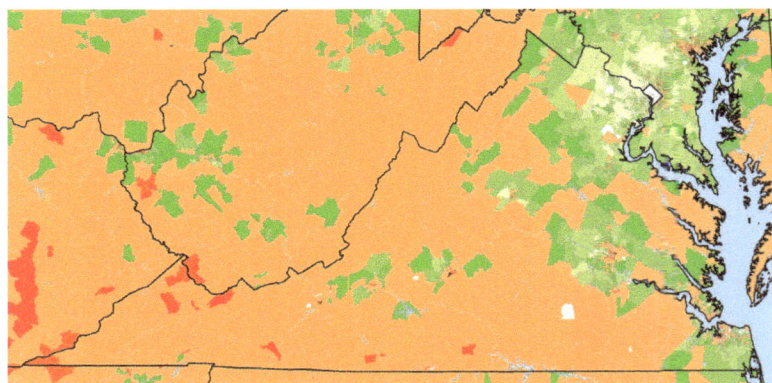

LEGEND

- 0.9% and below
- 0.9% to 1.4%
- 1.4% to 1.8%
- 1.8% to 2.2%
- 2.2% to 2.6%
- 2.6% to 3.0%
- 3.0% to 5.0%
- 5.0% to 7.5%
- 7.5% to 10%
- 10% and above
- Other

Washington

As of 2014, the average annual expenditures on electricity in Washington were $1,045 or 1.77 percent of the 2014 median household income of $59,068. The cost burden ranges from a low of 0.62 percent in parts of King County (median household income of $185,333), to a high of 11.88 percent in low-income parts of King County (median household income of $5,938).

2014 EXPENDITURES AS A PERCENTAGE OF MEDIAN HOUSEHOLD INCOME

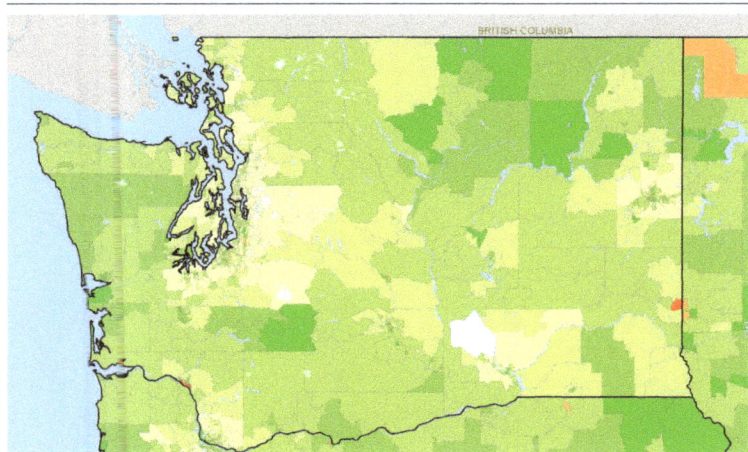

If the CPP is implemented, and consumers do not change their behavior, the cost burden will increase significantly to an average of $1,179 or 2.00 percent of 2014 median household income. In the high-income parts of King County, the burden increases to 0.69 percent, while in the low-income parts of King County the burden increases to 13.40 percent.

EXPENDITURES AS A PERCENTAGE OF MEDIAN HOUSEHOLD INCOME: STATIC ANALYSIS

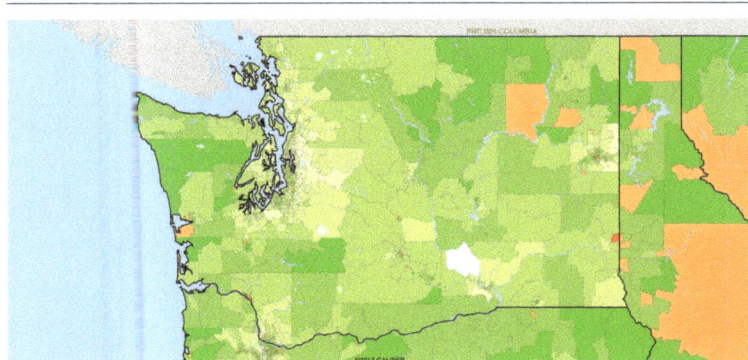

LEGEND

- 0.9% and below
- 0.9% to 1.4%
- 1.4% to 1.8%
- 1.8% to 2.2%
- 2.2% to 2.6%
- 2.6% to 3.0%
- 3.0% to 5.0%
- 5.0% to 7.5%
- 7.5% to 10%
- 10% and above
- Other

If consumers economize on their electricity consumption following the implementation of the CPP, the cost burden will increase but by less than under the static scenario. Based on the historical response in the short-term, average expenditures will increase to $1,153 or 1.95 percent of 2014 median household income − 0.68 percent in parts of King County and 13.11 percent in the low-income parts of King County.

EXPENDITURES AS A PERCENTAGE OF MEDIAN HOUSEHOLD INCOME: SHORT-TERM

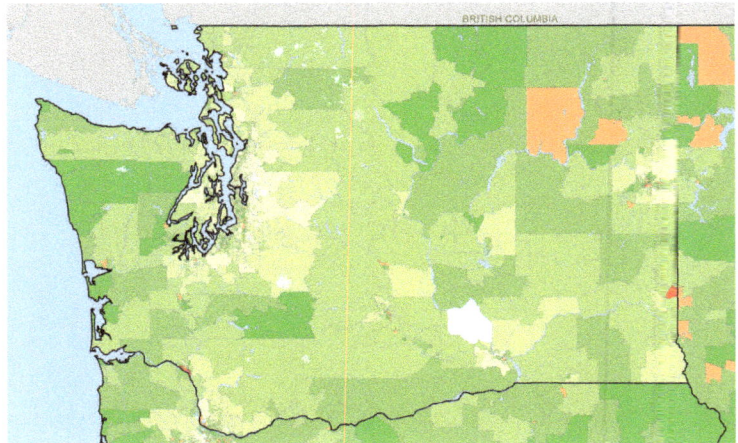

Based on the historical response in the long-term, average expenditures will increase to $1,145 or 1.94 percent of 2014 median household income − 0.67 percent in the upper-income parts of King County and 13.01 percent in the lower-income parts of King County.

EXPENDITURES AS A PERCENTAGE OF MEDIAN HOUSEHOLD INCOME: LONG-TERM

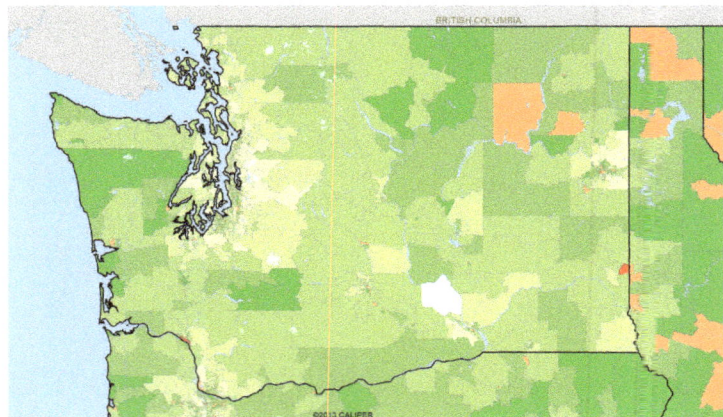

LEGEND

- 0.9% and below
- 0.9% to 1.4%
- 1.4% to 1.8%
- 1.8% to 2.2%
- 2.2% to 2.6%
- 2.6% to 3.0%
- 3.0% to 5.0%
- 5.0% to 7.5%
- 7.5% to 10%
- 10% and above
- Other

West Virginia

As of 2014, the average annual expenditures on electricity in West Virginia were $1,294 or 3.27 percent of the 2014 median household income of $39,552. The cost burden ranges from a low of 1.33 percent in parts of Kanawha County (median household income of $108,077), to a high of 10.92 percent in low-income parts of Cabell County (median household income of $8,003).

2014 EXPENDITURES
AS A PERCENTAGE OF
MEDIAN HOUSEHOLD
INCOME

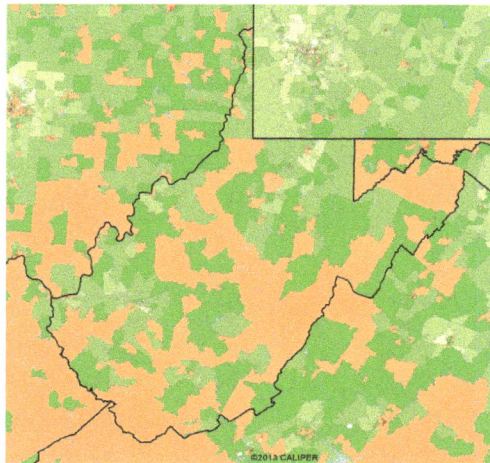

If the CPP is implemented, and consumers do not change their behavior, the cost burden will increase significantly to an average of $1,680 or 4.25 percent of 2014 median household income. In the high-income parts of Kanawha County, the burden increases to 1.72 percent, while in the low-income parts of Cabell County the burden increases to 14.17 percent.

EXPENDITURES AS
A PERCENTAGE OF
MEDIAN HOUSEHOLD
INCOME:
STATIC ANALYSIS

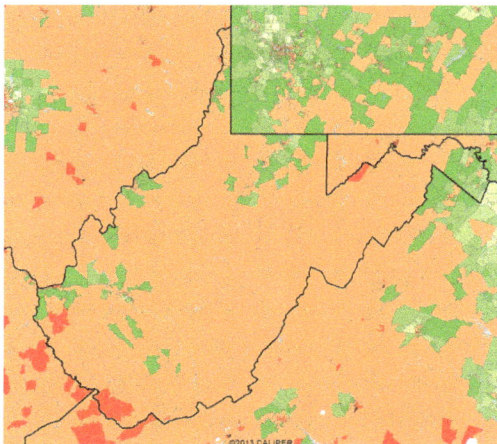

"The diversity of our energy mix is one of the reasons America currently enjoys affordable and reliable electricity. Competition not only keeps prices low; it also stimulates innovation, encourages economic growth and creates good-paying jobs across this great country."

—Senator
Joe Manchin (D-WV)

FACT

West Virginia families could soon be paying $1,680 a year on average for electricity under the Obama climate agenda.

LEGEND

- 0.9% and below
- 0.9% to 1.4%
- 1.4% to 1.8%
- 1.8% to 2.2%
- 2.2% to 2.6%
- 2.6% to 3.0%
- 3.0% to 5.0%
- 5.0% to 7.5%
- 7.5% to 10%
- 10% and above
- Other

If consumers economize on their electricity consumption following the implementation of the CPP, the cost burden will increase but by less than under the static scenario. Based on the historical response in the short-term, average expenditures will increase to $1,557 or 3.94 percent of 2014 median household income − 1.60 percent in parts of Kanawha County and 13.14 percent in the low-income parts of Cabell County.

EXPENDITURES AS A PERCENTAGE OF MEDIAN HOUSEHOLD INCOME: SHORT-TERM

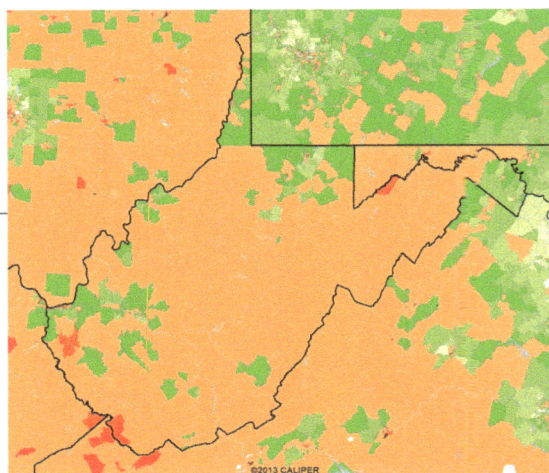

Based on the historical response in the long-term, average expenditures will increase to $1,544 or 3.90 percent of 2014 median household income − 1.58 percent in the upper-income parts of Kanawha County and 13.03 percent in the lower-income parts of Cabell County.

EXPENDITURES AS A PERCENTAGE OF MEDIAN HOUSEHOLD INCOME: LONG-TERM

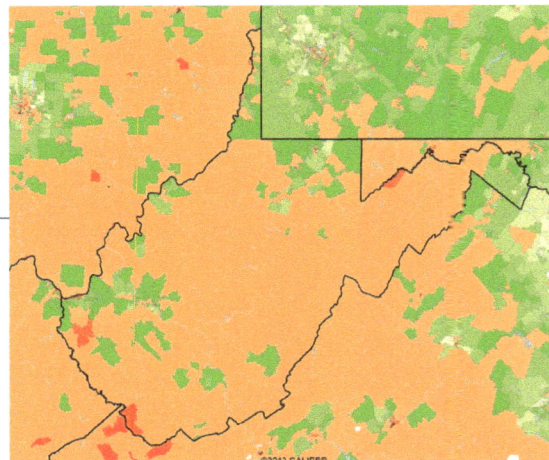

LEGEND

0.9% and below
0.9% to 1.4%
1.4% to 1.8%
1.8% to 2.2%
2.2% to 2.6%
2.6% to 3.0%
3.0% to 5.0%
5.0% to 7.5%
7.5% to 10%
10% and above
Other

Wisconsin

As of 2014, the average annual expenditures on electricity in Wisconsin were $1,140 or 1.96 percent of the 2014 median household income of $58,080. The cost burden ranges from a low of 0.70 percent in parts of Milwaukee County (median household income of $179,318), to a high of 8.96 percent in low-income parts of Dane County (median household income of $8,596).

2014 EXPENDITURES AS A PERCENTAGE OF MEDIAN HOUSEHOLD INCOME

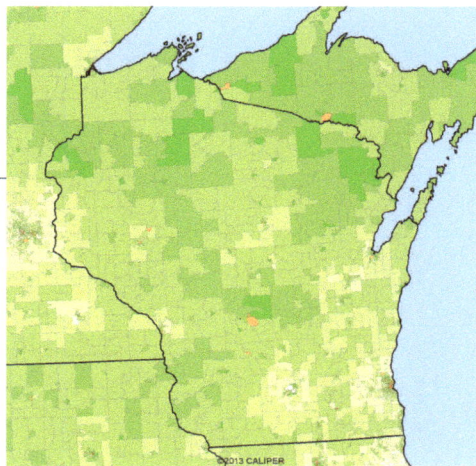

If the CPP is implemented, and consumers do not change their behavior, the cost burden will increase significantly to an average of $1,452 or 2.50 percent of 2014 median household income. In the high-income parts of Milwaukee County, the burden increases to 0.90 percent, while in the low-income parts of Dane County the burden increases to 11.40 percent.

EXPENDITURES AS A PERCENTAGE OF MEDIAN HOUSEHOLD INCOME: STATIC ANALYSIS

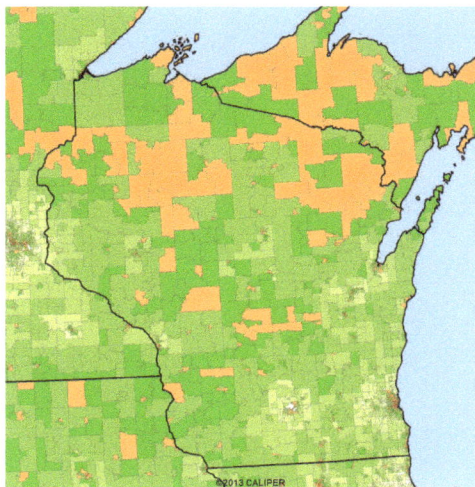

FACTS

- Wisconsin families could soon see their power bills rise to $1,452 a year on average under new Washington regulations.

- Low-income families in Dane County could see average electricity expenditures rise to 11.40 percent of their annual income.

- Bayfield County residents could see their power bills rise by 21.6 percent annually, while Milwaukee County residents could see their bills jump 21.5 percent.

LEGEND

- 0.9% and below
- 0.9% to 1.4%
- 1.4% to 1.8%
- 1.8% to 2.2%
- 2.2% to 2.6%
- 2.6% to 3.0%
- 3.0% to 5.0%
- 5.0% to 7.5%
- 7.5% to 10%
- 10% and above
- Other

If consumers economize on their electricity consumption following the implementation of the CPP, the cost burden will increase but by less than under the static scenario. Based on the historical response in the short-term, average expenditures will increase to $1,401 or 2.41 percent of 2014 median household income – 0.87 percent in parts of Milwaukee County and 11.00 percent in the low-income parts of Dane County.

EXPENDITURES AS A
PERCENTAGE OF MEDIAN
HOUSEHOLD INCOME:
SHORT-TERM

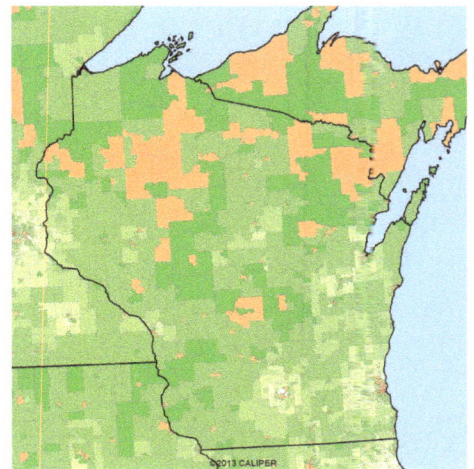

Based on the historical response in the long-term, average expenditures will increase to $1,376 or 2.37 percent of 2014 median household income – 0.85 percent in the upper-income parts of Milwaukee County and 10.81 percent in the lower-income parts of Dane County.

LEGEND

0.9% and below
0.9% to 1.4%
1.4% to 1.8%
1.8% to 2.2%
2.2% to 2.6%
2.6% to 3.0%
3.0% to 5.0%
5.0% to 7.5%
7.5% to 10%
10% and above
Other

EXPENDITURES AS A
PERCENTAGE OF MEDIAN
HOUSEHOLD INCOME: LONG-
TERM

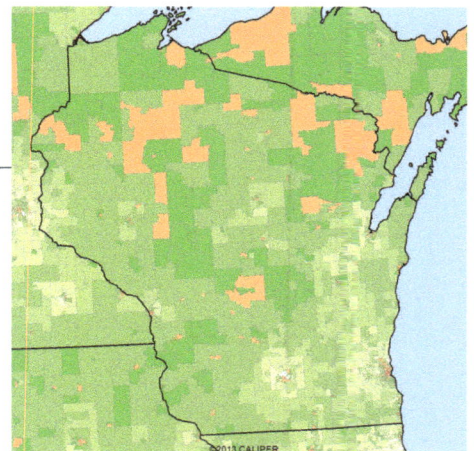

Wyoming

As of 2014, the average annual expenditures on electricity in Wyoming were $1,084 or 1.95 percent of the 2014 median household income of $55,690. The cost burden ranges from a low of 1.16 percent in parts of Laramie County (median household income of $103,203), to a high of 4.63 percent in low-income parts of Albany County (median household income of $15,804).

2014 EXPENDITURES AS A PERCENTAGE OF MEDIAN HOUSEHOLD INCOME

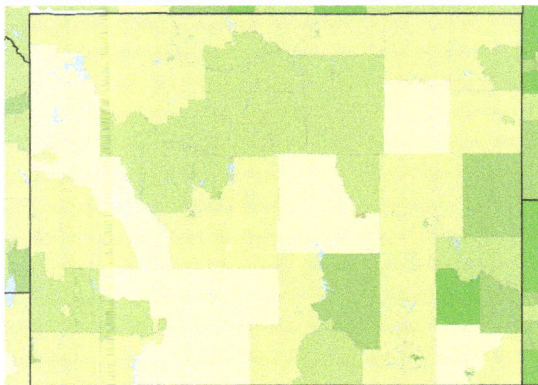

If the CPP is implemented, and consumers do not change their behavior, the cost burden will increase significantly to an average of $1,294 or 2.32 percent of 2014 median household income. In the high-income parts of Laramie County, the burden increases to 1.39 percent, while in the low-income parts of Albany County the burden increases to 5.53 percent.

EXPENDITURES AS A PERCENTAGE OF MEDIAN HOUSEHOLD INCOME: STATIC ANALYSIS

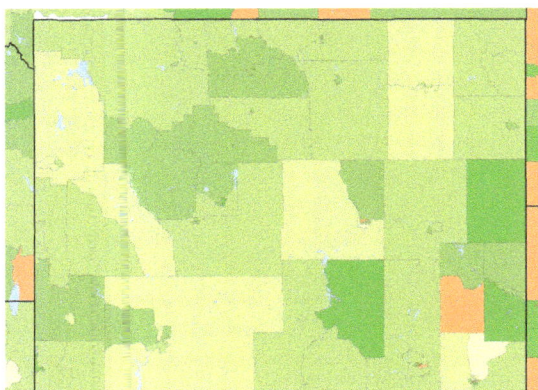

FACTS

- Wyoming families could soon be paying nearly $1,300 a year on average for electricity under the Obama climate agenda.

- For low-income communities in Albany County, the Clean Power Plan could increase average electricity expenditures to 5.53 percent of their annual household income.

- Sublette and Goshen County residents could see their power bills go up by 16.4 percent annually.

LEGEND

- 0.9% and below
- 0.9% to 1.4%
- 1.4% to 1.8%
- 1.8% to 2.2%
- 2.2% to 2.6%
- 2.6% to 3.0%
- 3.0% to 5.0%
- 5.0% to 7.5%
- 7.5% to 10%
- 10% and above
- Other

If consumers economize on their electricity consumption following the implementation of the CPP, the cost burden will increase but by less than under the static scenario. Based on the historical response in the short-term, average expenditures will increase to $1,249 or 2.24 percent of 2014 median household income – 1.34 percent in parts of Laramie County and 5.34 percent in the low-income parts of Albany County.

EXPENDITURES AS A PERCENTAGE OF MEDIAN HOUSEHOLD INCOME: SHORT-TERM

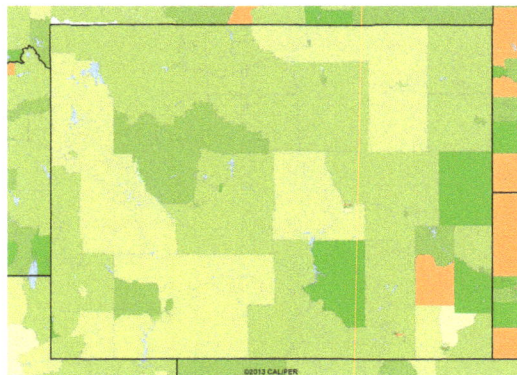

Based on the historical response in the long-term, average expenditures will increase to $1,238 or 2.22 percent of 2014 median household income – 1.33 percent in the upper-income parts of Laramie County and 5.29 parts of Albany County.

EXPENDITURES AS A PERCENTAGE OF MEDIAN HOUSEHOLD INCOME: LONG-TERM

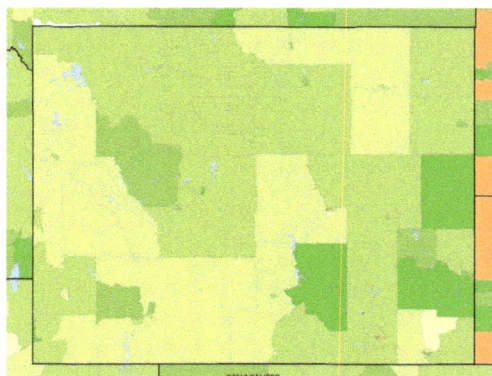

LEGEND

	0.9% and below
	0.9% to 1.4%
	1.4% to 1.8%
	1.8% to 2.2%
	2.2% to 2.6%
	2.6% to 3.0%
	3.0% to 5.0%
	5.0% to 7.5%
	7.5% to 10%
	10% and above
	Other